To Rachel Hope Green

Although your father never had a chance to hold you in his arms on earth—he holds you in his heart in Heaven.

—Mom

A PERSONAL NOTE
FROM MELODY

Keith Green was my husband for nearly nine years. I watched him close up as he struggled to follow Jesus without compromise. In the process he bumped into the same struggles we all face: How do we live "in the world" and not be "of the world" in the process? And when the world tells us to compromise—in all too convincing ways—how do we maintain our fiery passion for Jesus, our integrity, our purity?

I think the biggest question Keith tried to answer was one we all ask: What does it mean to be a true disciple of Jesus today? Keith would say, "We can't serve Jesus and the world at the same time. Jesus is coming back for a spotless bride. What bridegroom wants to marry someone who's messing around with someone else on the side?"

Keith and I were married in 1973 on Christmas day. By the spring of 1975, we had given our lives to Jesus. A few years later, Keith's musical talent propelled him to the top of the Christian charts. His soul-searching songs, coupled with his passionate and powerful delivery, are still changing lives around the world today.

But in spite of the legendary catalog of music Keith left behind, all that he had to say was not captured in his recordings alone. He had a brilliantly gifted mind and an intense desire to see God honored—and he didn't mind talking about it!

If you ever went to one of Keith's concerts, you quickly found out he was not shy about speaking his mind, whether people agreed with him or not. Between songs he'd often pace back and forth across the stage, looking out over the audience with focused intensity. He didn't mince words or try to ingratiate himself. He never felt compelled to make the audience feel warm and fuzzy about their faith. Instead, Keith challenged them to live a life that reflected what they said they believed. A different kind of life. A bold and uncompromising life lived for God. And when Keith spoke, you knew he spoke from his heart. You could see that God was dealing with him, just like God is dealing with you.

Keith's voice was strong, persistent, and hard to ignore. He spoke the truth we needed to hear then—and still need to hear now. In the brief seven years Keith knew Jesus, he trumpeted a wake-up call to Christians everywhere. "It's time to quit *playing* church," he often said, "and start *being* the church."

Sometimes Keith held up an uncomfortable standard. But he was also willing to be misunderstood and suffer rejection for his convictions. He used to say, "I've never tried to be controversial. The *truth* is controversial enough!" He simply believed the biblical premise that we're either hot or cold—that if we don't sell out to Jesus, we're certain to sell out to the world.

By his own admission there were times Keith could have seasoned his preaching with a bit more grace. But his powerful message has shaken hundreds of thousands of people into a more holy and radical devotion to Jesus Christ. There has been, and continues to be, eternal fruit from his life and ministry.

Besides his message to Christians, Keith was also an irrepressible evangelist. He not only led people to the Lord by the thousands at his concerts, he also led them one by one in restaurants, at the beach, in the woods, and in our living room! He even went door to door inviting our neighbors to our potluck Bible studies. He asked if they needed prayer—and gave them our phone number in case they might need prayer or some help later. Many new believers had nowhere to go, so we began taking them into our home in Southern California. Our small three-bedroom house began to burst at the seams. With money earned from Keith's concerts and our songwriters' salary from CBS Records, we bought a second house and rented five others in our neighborhood.

Soon we were a bustling community with about 70 new believers living in our seven homes—single moms, bikers, ex-druggies, and lots of young people like us who'd given up eastern mystical paths to embrace Jesus. They were all hungry and needed to be fed physically and spiritually. To keep our stomachs full we ate lots of weird, donated food, usually from unlabeled cans, but it was Keith who kept our spirits fed.

One of Keith's favorite things to do was to teach Bible studies, and he often taught several nights a week. He would plop down on the living room floor cross-legged and barefoot, open his Bible, and begin to preach like there was no tomorrow! He was spurred on by the sea of faces before him, hungry to learn about God. Most of the people had little or no understanding about what it meant to follow Jesus, and it was Keith's joy to teach them. Friends from church and even neighbors began to fill our living room for his worship times and Bible studies.

As we continued to grow and disciple new believers, we quickly became a recognized ministry. So in 1977 we gave ourselves a name—Last Days Ministries—and became a legal nonprofit ministry. Then in 1979 we moved to a 140-acre ranch in the hills of East Texas with lots of room to expand. Keith taught regularly, his teachings were always powerful yet practical as he opened the Word to us with humor, insight, and wisdom. We learned about living 100-percent sold-out lives—counting the cost, picking up our cross, prayer, suffering—and giving Jesus total lordship of our lives. Perhaps the most important lesson we learned was God's amazing love for us and our privilege of sharing God's love with others.

Keith taught some of the best Bible studies I've ever heard, literally hundreds of them. For this book I gathered his teachings together and transcribed, edited, and organized a virtual mountain of tapes. This book reflects only a portion of the messages gleaned, but over the next few years there will hopefully be other books that draw from Keith's powerful teaching ministry.

There are many Christians now with Jesus whose words were never published in their life-time—people like Oswald Chambers and Peter Marshall. Just as their teachings have enriched multitudes over the years, it's my prayer that this book will do the same. That's why we've taken such great care to preserve the integrity of Keith's messages, which seem more relevant today than ever.

During our marriage and ministry together, Keith's teachings impacted my life in an eternal way. I attended at least 95 percent of his studies, and a strong biblical foundation was laid in my life as a result. Today, more than ever, I see how Keith's teaching ministry helped prepare me for what I faced when the Lord took him home along with two of our small children, Josiah and Bethany. From the first moment of that 1982 plane crash, God began to carry me through the most devastating season of my life. I grew in my understanding of God's faithfulness and sovereignty. If Keith hadn't taught so often about the fact that sometimes we suffer in ways we don't understand, I wonder if my faith would have remained intact after such a tragedy. Little did I know that Keith's life would help prepare me for his death.

Keith's teachings will help lay a solid foundation in your life, too. They were born of the Spirit and so they are timeless. In fact, Last Days Ministries constantly gets requests for Keith's music and teachings as new people "discover" his ministry for the first time.

Today the Lord still speaks to us through the passionately intense voice of Keith Green. Keith challenged us to love God with our whole hearts and our whole lives. He called us to have a burning desire to see the Lord honored with all we have, all we say, and all we do. Keith believed everyone had a destiny to fulfill and that Jesus would empower us in mighty ways to impact our generation if we'd totally yield to him.

I pray that as you read this book your passion for Jesus will be ignited in a fresh way and that you'll fall more in love with him than ever before. I pray you'll make a new commitment to get hungrier for God, seek more of his presence, and love His Holy Spirit with greater abandon. As you read, open your heart and let the Lord speak his heart back to you.

I also pray that this book will help you discover your own unique voice. And when you do, I encourage you to speak boldly as the Lord leads you—whether it's sharing over a cup of coffee with friends, or, like Keith, in a voice that's heard around the world for years to come.

—Melody Green Sievright

1

CAN HE CALL
YOU "FRIEND"?

There's only one thing God could not have before he created us: friends. There was nobody to be his friend. Nobody to truly know him and in turn be known.

So God created us to share his heart, his thoughts, and his joy. Read in the Hebrew letter how God longed for friendship, fellowship, and relationship with us—how he hoped to know his people and for them to know him:

> This is the covenant I will make with the house of Israel after that time, declares the Lord. I will put my laws in their minds and write them on their hearts. I will be their God, and they will be my people. No longer will a man teach his neighbor, or a man his brother, saying, "Know the Lord" because they will all know me, from the least of them to the greatest.
>
> —HEBREWS 8:10-11

Can't you hear God cheering? "At last people will really know me! Old people, young people, rich people, poor people—everyone will know me personally instead of relying on others to tell them about me!"

Jesus announced that the new covenant, this new way of knowing God, had come at last. He said:

> I no longer call you servants because a servant does not know his master's business. Instead I have called you friends, for everything that I learned from my Father I have made known to you.
>
> —JOHN 15:15

Are you a friend to Jesus? How do you treat his desire for intimacy with you? Are you someone who fulfills the longing in his heart?

Or will he have this charge against you: "You are going through all the spiritual motions like an expert, but you've lost your first love. You've let your love run dry."

It's not too late to be the friend God desires. Ask him now—cry out to him: "God, set my heart on fire with real love for you!" Commit yourself to him. Don't let another day go by, not one more minute. He's waiting to say to you: "Well done, my friend."

2

BEYOND THE BLESS-ME CLUB

Being one of Jesus' first disciples couldn't have been easy. Christ continually challenged everyone's motives. In fact, one of his toughest questions, posed in Luke 6:46, haunts me: "Why do you call me, 'Lord, Lord,' and do not do what I say?"

Jesus throws out this challenge because he knows human nature. He knows that you and I want the security of friendship with him. We want his love and peace, plus the assurance that we're going to spend eternity with him.

He also knows that, in our human nature, we don't want it to cost us anything. We want something for nothing, sort of a personal "bless-me club."

But that's a one-way friendship. So his challenge brings us face-to-face with one of the great paradoxes of the gospel: Yes, salvation is God's free gift, but receiving that gift is going to cost us everything—our whole life. We must surrender our lives to him, let our old selves die so we can be born anew into his family.

That was Jesus' challenge to his disciples, and his challenge to us too.

Have you truly died to yourself? Who is ruling on the throne of your life? Are you still in command? It's Jesus asking, "Why do you call me, 'Lord, Lord,' and do not do what I say?"

3

BUILD A ROOM
WITH A HEAVENLY VIEW!

Remember Jesus' story about the wise builder and the foolish one? The wise man dug down deep, so he could build the foundation for his house on solid rock. The foolish man wanted to build his house quickly, so he built right on top of the sandy soil and didn't worry about anything else but getting ahead.

Now, if you build a house without worrying about the foundation, you're going to be finished building a long time before everyone else. In fact you're going to look pretty smart to passersby who see you relaxing on your balcony, watching the other guy still pounding nails and finishing the roof.

Onlookers probably will say, "Look at how fast he finished that place. He must really know something about building. That other guy must be crazy slogging away with so much sweat and effort for a house that looks just like this one that's already finished."

Then a storm comes. A flood washes away the house that went up fast because it wasn't built on a proper foundation. Meanwhile, the house on the solid foundation stands firm and rides out the storm.

Now who's the crazy one?

Isn't our faith like that? It's continually tempting to build faith quick and easy. Who wants to dig or work hard? Foundations aren't that pretty, anyway.

They aren't showy. People don't go by and say, "I just love your foundation." In fact, foundations usually aren't noticed.

Human nature wants to skip over the foundation altogether and go straight to the things people are going to see: the spectacular, public, high-profile things. For instance, if a pastor asks for someone to lead worship, he is flooded with volunteers. But when he asks for volunteers to clean the church bathrooms or work in the nursery, everyone is suddenly very busy.

Somehow we manage to find enough time to prepare to lead worship, but not enough time to help with a practical thing like cleaning a bathroom. Why? We all know the answer. Where's the fame? Where's the glamour? Where's the reward in cleaning a toilet for Jesus?

In our flesh we would rather seek the praises of people than of God. We want to put on an outward show. Why worry about a foundation of inner obedience and servanthood to the Lord? Jesus pointed out the answer: Without laying a solid foundation, we will be swept away by some storm of life. Everyone will see that what we did, no matter how impressive it looked at the time, was a work built on sand. It will be clear that we skimped on building proper foundations in our lives. Just like a man who starts to build a tower without counting his money to see if he has enough to finish it (Luke 14:28-30), or like the five foolish virgins who didn't take enough oil with them to make it until the bridegroom came (Matthew 25:1-13), we dare not start something in the name of the Lord without digging down deep before we build up. He doesn't want us left in ruins when the storms come. He wants us safe inside his well-built home with him.

4

How to Get
Off the Ground

When Melody and I were new Christians, all sorts of people came to our Bible studies. I'll never forget one guy in particular, a new believer, who came with every spiritual book imaginable, including a Bible, concordance, and *The Aquarian Gospel of Jesus Christ.*

I'd begin a Bible study and he'd take over, reading from all these other spiritual books. He spent hours telling us that to eat meat was of the devil, and he went on and on about other weird doctrines.

I lost touch with him for a long time, then saw him at a convention. He'd just come back from Israel, where he chanted on the streets. As I listened to his experiences, I thought, *Here's a brand-new believer who never got off the ground!* He couldn't discern false teaching and wouldn't listen to anyone who might help him. He was completely derailed. All kinds of seeds of darkness had been sown in him, and he had no way to fend them off.

We must learn to take the high road of faith and reject false teachings. Even when it's not popular, we must hold onto the truth. Remember Hebrews 13:8-9: "Jesus Christ is the same yesterday and today and forever. Do not be carried away by all kinds of strange teachings...."

In the end times we're going to experience false teachings that are doctrines of demons, and smooth-sounding teachings that are really from antichrists. There will be people close to becoming Christians, but who nevertheless are deceived. Our safeguard is in what the Hebrews were told: Listen only to teachers whose lives show the fruit of the Spirit, those who *do* what they *preach,* those who follow the true gospel.

5

Do You Hear
What Paul Heard?

Are you following the true gospel—the one Jesus preached, the one Paul and the other apostles heard and passed on to us? How do you know?

Most born-again Christians can see through heretical teachings. Some of those teachings are so far off the wall it's hard to believe anyone could take them seriously. Others are much more subtle and difficult to spot, especially when they are mixed in with what Jesus taught.

That's why Paul warns us about these other messages. He's even blunt: "I am astonished that you are so quickly deserting the one who called you by the grace of Christ and are turning to a different gospel—which is really no gospel at all. Evidently some people are throwing you into confusion and are trying to pervert the gospel of Christ" (Galatians 1:6-7).

See, in Paul's day other preachers had different types of gospels or "good news," which is what the word "gospel" means. Some preached that salvation could be achieved by eating the right foods or practicing strict personal disciplines. There was the Gnostic gospel, which was a type of early mysticism—the worship of many gods, and there were even so-called "messiahs" at the time of Christ.

Compare that to today's teachers of these other gospels, the ones who try to convince us things are not as black and white as Paul makes them out to be. These teachers tell us there is a little room to accommodate the flesh—that we can expect wealth and good health. They say the way pointed out in the Bible is just an ideal, goals we're meant to aim at but not expected to hit.

Things haven't changed have they? All these ideas are designed to appeal to our flesh, and Satan uses them to lull us until we're ineffective.

But Paul preached that the true gospel involved making tough choices and taking hard stands. Sometimes standing for the gospel means losing popularity with your friends, suffering for your convictions, and even putting your life on the line.

Paul himself lived through these challenges. After his encounter with Christ on the road to Damascus, he became a wanted man. Paul was hunted down by the same Pharisees who had been his friends and colleagues because he spoke against their "gospels," which were not the true gospel at all, but merely vain attempts to offer God the sort of religious practices he wasn't really interested in anyway. God isn't looking for religious rituals. He certainly isn't looking for religion. He wants to have an intimate heart-to-heart *relationship* with us. It's that simple.

6

SACRIFICING CONTROL

Following the gospel Jesus preached often calls for great sacrifice. Paul understood this. Imprisoned for his beliefs, he suffered torture and beatings; through the things endured, Paul showed he had the credentials to speak and teach with authority about the true gospel. He urged Timothy and the Galatians to be wary of a gospel that's more comfortable, a gospel that allows you to withhold your heart from God and offer him only a few trinkets. He explained to Timothy:

> [God's grace] has now been revealed through the appearing of our Savior, Christ Jesus, who has destroyed death and has brought life and immortality to light through the gospel. And of this gospel I was appointed a herald and an apostle and a teacher. That is why I am suffering as I am. Yet I am not ashamed, because I know whom I have believed, and am convinced that he is able to guard what I have entrusted to him for that day. What you heard from me, keep as the pattern of sound teaching, with faith and love in Christ Jesus. Guard the good deposit that was entrusted to you—guard it with the help of the Holy Spirit who lives in us.
>
> —2 TIMOTHY 1:10-14

Paul's warning is worth repeating. There are a lot of teachings out there that appeal to our flesh. They avoid sacrifice. They do not challenge us to give Jesus total control of our lives. They do not lead to salvation.

What God wants is *all* of you: heart, soul, mind, and body. He wants you to embrace him and his unconditional love. When you do, he gives you the strength you need to face any circumstance that comes your way. This was Paul's secret for enduring the trials he went through. Paul also realized, just as we need to, that this world was not his final home. God wants to use you to call the world back to him.

7

LIVE FOR HIM
LIKE YOU MEAN IT

Like the apostle Paul, Rees Howells found out God doesn't want us to play games. Howells was a preacher and leader in the great Welsh Revival of the early 1900s, and later in England, Ireland, and Africa. He insisted his effectiveness for Christ came from one incident when he was 27 years old, a life-changing encounter with the Holy Spirit three years after his surrender to Jesus. In the book *Rees Howells, Intercessor*, biographer Norman Grubb recounts the meeting with the Holy Spirit in Howell's own words:

> I saw Him as a person apart from flesh and blood and He said to me, "As the Savior had a body, so I dwell in the cleansed temple of the believer. I am God and I come to ask you to give your body to Me, that I may work through you. I need a body for my temple. But it must belong to me without reserve, for two persons with different wills can never live in the same body. Will you give Me yours? You must go out. I shall not mix Myself with yourself."
>
> I saw the honor He gave me in offering to indwell me but there were many things very dear to me and I knew He wouldn't keep even one of them. The

change He would make was very clear. It
meant every bit of my fallen nature was
to go to the cross, and He would bring
His own life and His own nature into me.
It was unconditional surrender.[1]

So God gave Howells an ultimatum: Would he obey
or not?

For the next few days, Howells wept continually. He
couldn't eat or sleep, and he lost seven pounds. This
was the most difficult decision he would ever have to
make—to hand over his life like a blank check to God.
Was he willing to let go of all his dreams and possessions, and let the Holy Spirit take full control? He
could no longer toy with a decision. His biography
records:

> The Holy Spirit went on dealing with
> me, exposing the root of my nature,
> which was self. You can only get out of a
> thing what is in its root. Sin was can-
> celled and it wasn't sin He was dealing
> with; it was self, that thing which came
> from the Fall. He was not going to take
> any superficial surrender. He put His
> finger on each part of my self-life, and I
> [had] to decide in cold blood. He could
> never take a thing away until I gave my
> consent.[2]

In order to receive the resurrection life, and power
that goes along with it, we must be willing to let go of
everything we hold close. Sometimes our flesh screams
as we do this. Other times it devises subtle ways of getting us off-track, quietly distracting us with side
issues—anything to keep us from giving everything to
God. Suddenly small matters of theology become
major issues as we focus on anything but what the
Holy Spirit wants us to deal with. There comes a time

when the Spirit puts his finger on specific areas in our lives and asks us to hand over all control to him.

Rees Howells surrendered to the Holy Spirit's challenge. When God gives *you* an ultimatum, what will you do?

1. Norman Grubb, *Rees Howells, Intercessor* (Fort Washington, PA.: Christian Literature Crusade, 1967), pp. 38-40.

2. Ibid.

8

FIND YOUR FOCUS

Have you ever noticed how easily small children can be distracted? Give children candy and you can walk off with all their toys. For a while they'll be so happy with the candy they won't even notice.

Believers can be like that, too. Paul continually reminded the Christians of his day to stay on-track. If they did not stay focused on Jesus, other preachers would come along to lead them astray with their fleshly gospels. Some people concentrated on getting rich quick, like Simon the sorcerer in Acts 8:9-25. Others sought to turn the gospel into a purely mystical experience. Yet others wanted to bog down the whole message in Jewish laws and customs.

After a few months, if these young Christians hadn't received a letter from Paul, they probably would have begun to listen to these other messages. They wanted to see if other interpretations of the Christian life were easier to follow. Their flesh kept tempting them to believe many things that weren't the gospel of the kingdom, despite their hunger for spiritual truth and Paul's strong warnings:

> But even if we or an angel from heaven should preach a gospel other than the one we preached to you, let him be eternally condemned! As we have already said, so now I say again: If anybody is

preaching to you a gospel other than
what you accepted, let him be eternally
condemned! Am I now trying to win the
approval of men, or of God? Or am I
trying to please men? If I were still trying
to please men, I would not be a servant of
Christ.

—GALATIANS 1:8-10

We are no different. I once heard a prophecy that
the city of Chicago was going to be leveled by an
earthquake on a particular day. I thought, *I'll believe
it when I see it.* But a couple of young Christians I
worked with got really excited.

"What time will it hit?" one of them asked me. He
was so trusting.

"I have an uncle in Chicago," another one said.
"I'm going to call him and tell him to get out before
it's too late."

I can understand their concern because there
was a time when I used to look for big signs, too. I
was swayed by the gospel of sensationalism and
easily led astray. I believed things that were not doc-
trinally sound.

Here's the point: Each one of us must take
responsibility before God to keep our eyes on the
gospel. We can't allow anything or anyone to distract
or mislead us.

9

THE DEAD HAVE NO RIGHTS

Paul wrote to Timothy, "Here is a trustworthy saying: If we died with him, we will also live with him" (2 Timothy 2:11). That's the heart of the gospel. You must die with Christ in order to live with him. But what exactly does it mean?

For starters it means you are to be dead to your rights. That means signing over to God your desires, dreams, hurts, and all that you are or will be.

What else do you think Paul meant when he said, "For you died, and your life is now hidden with Christ in God" (Colossians 3:3)? He wasn't talking about a theory or a nice metaphor. He meant that at the point of real salvation you are nailed to the cross with Jesus. You go down to the grave and a new life, God's life, is born in you.

What I'm talking about at the deepest level is an exchange of wills: I give my will over to God and begin to pursue his will for me.

So why do a lot of people get stuck on certain behavior—old habits, for instance? Probably because it's easy to give up your wrongs, but much more difficult to give up your rights. The temptation is to clean up the flesh without becoming pure in heart first. But we become pure in heart by wanting what God wants.

For me, as a Christian, that means having no rights. Have you ever heard of a dead person calling from the grave for a lawyer to sue someone for violating his rights? See, the dead have no rights. So I have no right to run a ministry or even own a car. But in Christ I do have the right to inherit all of God's promises in the Bible—if I can prove to myself, to the world, and to Jesus that I am dead.

10

THE POWER IN "IF"

Here's a promise most of us might not want to claim: "If we endure, we will also reign with him. If we disown him, he will also disown us" (2 Timothy 2:12).

The "if" is a crucial part. People who follow the wrong gospel want to make the "ifs" invisible. They like to think there are no conditions in the Bible.

True, God's love is not conditional. But there is a condition on experiencing the true life of Christ. It is giving over our will. That means we stop manipulating God's Word for our own gain.

Have you died with Christ? Or are you trying to live with him at the same time you're doing everything to accommodate your own desires?

The Holy Spirit doesn't want the flesh for a roommate. God requires a choice. You cannot have your life and the life of Christ residing in you at the same time. The problem for most of us is that we want a spiritual crown, yet we also want to avoid the cross that must come first. Something has to give.

Paul told Timothy, "*If* we endure, we will also reign with him" (2 Timothy 2:12, emphasis added).

When people read this they think: *Yes! I'm going to live with Christ.* They think God is going to endure for them. They sit back and act as if God will do all the work.

Mistakenly they ignore the "if."

The "if" is important, though. It's like a spotlight Paul turns on you. You are to endure by casting everything—hopes and cares alike—upon God. That's your work in faith: to identify every fleshly goal or care that draws you away from God and cast it all over to him, dying to him. After all, faith is not just hope. Faith is a deed. It's active, not passive. It's claiming: "God and me in partnership. First his will replaces mine, then his power enables me to do all that he says."

It's when you do his will that God blesses you because you cannot be spiritually blessed in a place where his will does not reign.

11

GOD PREPARES YOU
TO ENDURE

If you're going to endure, to choose the high road of faith, then you have to be prepared for some attacks. So you don't get weary and give up, you might as well know this from the start: Be prepared. Count the cost. Peter says:

> Be self-controlled and alert. Your enemy the devil prowls around like a roaring lion looking for someone to devour. Resist him, standing firm in the faith, because you know that your brothers throughout the world are undergoing the same kind of sufferings.
> —1 PETER 5:8-9

See, apart from God, Satan is the most powerful being in the universe. Like a lion on the prowl he looks for unsuspecting Christians to chew up. He's inflamed with pride, jealousy, greed, and the power God has allowed him to keep. So your conflict is not against flesh and blood, but against this ruler of the darkness.

That's why God gives you spiritual weapons for the fight: truth, salvation, and prayer (Ephesians 6:10-20). When you choose God's will, you're guaranteed the power of the Holy Spirit in order to endure the assaults of the devil.

12

THE COMFORT
OF BEING UNSETTLED

We know we're truly following Jesus if we learn to endure the attacks of Satan, resist false teachings, and overcome the lusts of the flesh. By that I mean learning to live free from all the things that seek to bind us to this world.

John warned against "the lust of the eyes and the boasting of what he has and does" (1 John 2:16); Paul warned us to flee from immorality (1 Corinthians 6:18) and pursue righteousness (2 Timothy 2:22). A lot of Christians know how to flee. They get out of the world. But they don't know how to pursue righteousness and get the world out of them.

Paul told us how: Set your affections on things above (Colossians 3:1). Not only are we supposed to be turning away *from* something, he said we're supposed to turn heart, soul, body, and mind *toward* something. That something is described in Philippians 3:14: "the prize for which God has called me heavenward"—to be like Jesus in this world.

Like Paul, I want to be found growing in the image and likeness of Jesus Christ. When God calls me home or when Jesus comes back, whichever comes first, I want to be a true disciple, one who set his affections on the wonderful things above. That means letting go of all that this world offers by way of security, honor, and pleasure.

That's how I know if I'm following the gospel.

The gospel will challenge us at every turn. It will unsettle us, and require things of us that hurt and make our flesh squirm. The devil will attack our weakest areas. Other Christians will offer us less radical ways to follow Christ, but in the end we'll be transformed from the inside out. We'll be clean. We'll be shining lights to people who are broken and hurting and don't know the love of Jesus. Then we'll be known by the fruit of the Spirit in our lives. We will know we are truly his disciples.

13

THE SECRET
TO BEARING FRUIT

Charles Finney led the great Christian revival that swept through America during the nineteenth century. He seemed to feel the urgency of John the Baptist's words, "...every tree that does not produce good fruit will be cut down and thrown into the fire" (Matthew 3:10). So, like John the Baptist, Finney was considered a radical by some, and, like John, he set his world on fire with the gospel.

What did Finney know about converting souls to Christ that too many of us miss?

When Finney came into a town he held what he called an "anxious inquirer's meeting" for people worried about the state of their souls. Finney didn't preach at these meetings. He simply got up and said that to receive salvation one needed to repent and be forgiven, then he quietly exited the room. No manipulating. No emotional pitch. No pressure.

Left alone with God, people wept. They came under tremendous conviction of sin as the Holy Spirit dealt with them. They begged God to have mercy on them.

You'd think a revivalist preacher would jump on this, wouldn't you?

Not Finney. Instead of leading these crying people through the sinner's prayer, he would send them home for the night. Finney wasn't interested in false or premature conversions. He believed sinners needed to be so deeply convicted of their sin that they turned from their old lives to pursue God with every ounce of strength.

That's just what happened—and more. Few of the many thousands who came to the Lord under Finney's ministry ever backslid.

How did he do it? He didn't. He knew the Holy Spirit would work in the hearts of people. It's not a Christian's job to bring a person to repentance and new life in Christ. Finney understood this and was careful not to rob the Spirit of his role. But Finney took his job seriously: Go and, like a good tree bears fruit, do the Christian's job—bear the good news to others.

14

TELL EVERYTHING
YOU KNOW

Why would anyone give up the Christian life after putting their hand to the plow? Some do, you know. Through any given ministry, only one-fourth of the people who come to the Lord go on with God and don't backslide.

This may be because we haven't told people everything we know about salvation.

Repentance is the condition of salvation, but we neglect to talk about it. It has become an option, not a requirement. Yet I can't find one place in Scripture where God offers forgiveness before repentance.

Jesus told a crowd of both religious leaders and ordinary folks: "I tell you, no! But unless you repent, you too will all perish" (Luke 13:3).

His disciples passed on the same sobering message. Mark said, "They went out and preached that people should repent" (Mark 6:12).

Peter, standing up on the day of Pentecost, preached, "Repent and be baptized, every one of you in the name of Jesus Christ for the forgiveness of your sins..." (Acts 2:38).

Paul said, "First to those of Damascus, then to those in Jerusalem and in all Judea, and to the Gentiles also, I preached that they should repent and turn to God and prove their repentance by their deeds" (Acts 26:20).

God's offer is always the same, whether it's to the Jews, Christians in the early church, or people we meet today: If we repent of our sin, we will be forgiven. Why settle for less in our spiritual lives—less power, less love, less fruit?

15

THE REAL DEAL

Let's face it. A lot of preachers today sound more like used-car salesmen than ministers of the gospel. It's as if they're selling Christianity as the ultimate ride: "Do you want to be rid of all your worries? Do you want to have joy? Peace? Happiness? Get rid of all the problems in your life? Then step right up and receive Jesus! Say 'yes' to him now!"

The sinner who hears this thinks: *Yeah, I want all that. I want joy and peace. I want to know I'm going to heaven. I want to feel like I did when I won the trip to Hawaii. And all I've got to do is say "yes"? It's the deal of the century!*

So people run forward to answer altar calls. Someone leads them in a sinner's prayer, which you can't find anywhere in Scripture. Then each person responding is handed a Bible and told to read it once a day and pray. Each trusting soul gets a pat on the back and someone says: "Praise the Lord! You're born again! You're a Christian now!"

But did anyone hear about repentance?

Too often not. So these people go home and for the first few days everything is great. They feel joyful and happy, just like when they won that trip to Hawaii. They read their Bibles and pray, just like they were told. Then things start coming apart. Their bosses get mad at them. Their cars get scratched. Their dog gets run over. Their investments don't pay. Old friends drop them.

Pretty soon they're back where they started. They wonder, *Where is all this peace I was promised?* and *Where's the blessing?* And finally, *Is God even real?*

That's when these people may turn their backs and walk away. They didn't find the easy, happy lives they were looking for, and we Christians failed to tell them that the ultimate goal of accepting Christ is not to be happy every minute of the day.

Now I'm not for Christians going around with long faces, but the Bible isn't filled with stories of God making people happy. It's filled with stories of God making people holy.

And there's a long process involved in making people holy. It takes time. It isn't comfortable. Sometimes it downright hurts. But if we're patient and cooperate with God, we will reap the benefits of his work in our lives. We may not always know happiness, but we can have his peace throughout the process.

Besides, are we really more interested in signatures on a decision card than in making sure we've told all we know about receiving forgiveness and growing into children of God?

16

WHO'S SORRY NOW?

I think most sinners are sorry for their sins. I abused drugs for three years and was sorry the whole time: sorry about what I was doing to myself, sorry I was caught in a trap. But being sorry never got me out of the snare of drug abuse.

Prisoners are sorry too—sorry they're in prison! Prison ministers will tell you a lot of inmates say: "I'm sorry about the state my life's in. When I get out of here I'm going straight." But feeling sorry isn't enough to turn around their lives. The next time they get caught and end up back in jail, they'll be sorry again.

Like revivalist Charles Finney said, "If repentance means feeling sorry about sin, then hell is filled with repentant people."

See, when it comes to repentance, feeling sorry for your sins isn't enough. Jesus, Peter, Paul, and the rest of the disciples said repentance means: Change the way you think about God and sin. Realign your feelings and actions. Choose to hate sin and love God. See the pain and destruction your sin has brought to God, other people, and yourself. Then forsake sin and live a life that's pleasing to God.

Finney put it this way: "Repentance is a change of willing, of feeling, and of living in respect to God."

This is hard. But repentance is not lip service. Repentance is seeing the blackness of our sin, and saying to God: "I realize how much pain I've caused you. My sin helped drive the nails into your flesh and bones." It's only when we see that our sin cost him blood that we can turn away from ourselves and willingly live to please God.

That's why John the Baptist said we need to produce fruit in keeping with repentance (Matthew 3:8). That's why Paul reminded the people he preached to that they should prove their repentance by their deeds (Acts 26:20).

Repentance has to come from the heart. When it does, it produces tangible evidence to God, yourself, and those around you that you have truly repented because your life has changed.

17

HOW TO COME CLEAN
WITH GOD

A young woman named MaryAnn lived for some time in one of our homes. She confided that her father had sexually abused her as a child. But since becoming a Christian, she said it didn't bother her anymore. She'd forgiven her father for what he'd done to her. She even wrote him a letter to tell him so. She told us: "I've forgiven him. I'm fine with God."

Everything seemed nice, neat, and sweet.

Then praying one day MaryAnn closed her eyes and saw her father's face. Immediately she felt tremendous hate for him, such rage that for the first time she knew in her heart she'd mentally murdered her father many times for what he'd done to her.

The Holy Spirit was showing MaryAnn the real condition of her heart. For so long she'd tried to pretend she didn't hate her father because she was a Christian—and Christians don't feel hate, right? Yet this hatred was affecting her relationship with her heavenly Father. With God's help, MaryAnn broke through the despair to discover true repentance. She realized the pain her hatred had caused in her life as she gained a deeper insight into how sin separates us from God.

That was when MaryAnn's pain over what was in her heart finally came out. She wept and wept, then immediately wrote her father another letter. This time she asked him to forgive her for her hatred and unwillingness to forgive him in her own heart. She realized if she continued in bitterness she would be eaten away by it. This did not in any way condone her father's sin or release him from its consequences. But MaryAnn's true repentance gave her father an opportunity to witness Christ's love at work and, perhaps, helped her dad be more open to the work of the Holy Spirit in his own life. It also lifted a burden MaryAnn had carried for years.

Do you see what I'm driving at? It's so easy to whitewash your sins. So easy to bury them in some dark corner of your heart and hope nobody ever finds them. That's what MaryAnn did. She was only set free when the Holy Spirit shone his light into her heart so she could see the sin that was really there.

You see true repentance has to be a work of the Holy Spirit because we're blinded by our sin and think we're a lot better than we really are. Only God sees into every crevice of our hearts. He knows the garbage that's piled up there: selfishness, anger, jealousy, self-pity, lust, possessiveness. He wants us to see it as he does, and to decide we're going to get rid of it.

Until MaryAnn saw her hate, she could not repent of it. But because of her repentance she is free today and walking in victory. She discovered peace comes when you get honest with yourself about the sin that's piled up in your heart—and when you ask God to remove the filth. It's a matter of coming clean before the Lord.

18

THE RIGHT REPENTANCE

Do you understand the difference between the conviction of the Holy Spirit and the condemnation of the devil? If not, you probably rebuke the devil, do spiritual warfare, and wonder why nothing changes.

Maybe you haven't recognized that the Holy Spirit might be working hard to get your attention. Maybe he wants to show you the condition of your heart. Maybe he wants to point out sins hidden away in dark corners—sins you don't want to admit. But you can become free only when you own up to those sins and repent.

When I first came to the Lord, I didn't understand repentance at all. I spent a lot of time seeking counsel. "I don't feel saved," I'd tell my counselor. "There are so many areas where I'm failing, weak, and frustrated."

He would tell me, "That's the devil condemning you. You have to resist him and believe Jesus loves you."

"Yeah," I'd say, "but I'm rotten in all those areas, and I'm making a mess of things. I don't have any peace. How can I really be saved?"

"Of course you're saved," he'd tell me. "We all make mistakes sometimes. Don't listen to those lies. God says you are free now. Receive that by faith."

So every counseling session would end with me resolving to pray more and exercise more faith—and I would! I'd spend more time talking to God and reading my Bible every day. But one week later I was right back at the same spot.

One day I couldn't stand it any longer. "I don't care if I rot in here," I told Melody. "I'm not coming out of the house until I have the peace of God." I buried my face in my mattress and cried out to God with all my heart and soul: "Lord, I can't stand my hypocrisy anymore. I can't stand any longer acting like it's revival time in my heart when I have no peace. What's my problem?"

The Holy Spirit shined his light into my heart. "Don't you see?" he asked me. "Your pride has told you that your sin is just a part of your personality. Your pride has allowed you to believe these weak areas are something you'll have to learn to accept. That's not the truth. You are a sinner, and you need to repent."

"Yes, Lord," I said, "but we're all sinners!"

The Lord's rebuke stopped me in my tracks: "Don't make excuses. You are a sinner." Then He began to show me what I felt was His conviction.

Do you see? God was trying to lead me to repentance, and I'd been rebuking the devil instead! What I didn't know, because no one had told me, was how to embrace the whole message of salvation. I had not faced my sin and repented of it.

So many other Christians are in bondage because they haven't experienced true freedom either. No one has explained to them what repentance does for you. No one has told them about dealing ruthlessly with sin so they can be free from it at last. They've been advised, as I was, to use the word "faith" to mean "pretend." You know, to say, "I'm set free by faith," then pretend you're free when you aren't.

That's not faith; that's a sad joke. David gives insight on this:

> When I kept silent, my bones wasted away through my groaning all day long. For day and night your hand was heavy upon me; my strength was sapped as in the heat of summer. Then I acknowledged my sin to you and did not cover up my iniquity. I said, "I will confess my transgression to the LORD"—and you forgave the guilt of my sin.
>
> —PSALM 32:3-5

"Your hand was heavy upon me." That's conviction of sin; it led David to repent of his sin, confess it to the Lord, and receive forgiveness so his guilt was taken away.

See, the devil wants to demoralize you and ultimately destroy you. The Holy Spirit wants to convict you so you can repent and be restored. The difference is simple: The Holy Spirit is always specific. He says, "Quit yelling at your kids," or "Pray more." The devil is general in his accusations: "You're a terrible parent and a lousy, prayerless Christian. Why don't you just give up?"

Once you know who's talking, you can give the right response—and be free.

19

You Can Be Excused—Or Holy

What happens when you're faced with a conviction of the Holy Spirit and you begin to rebuke the devil instead of recognizing God at work?

Look at King Saul, who made excuses rather than repent. The prophet Samuel had delivered the word of the Lord to Saul: Fight against and utterly destroy the Amalekites, right down to their sheep, oxen, and goats. So Saul went to battle. But he was on a glory trip and decided to take captive Agag, the king of the Amalekites, to show off as a prisoner of war. Saul allowed his men to take the Amalekites' best sheep and oxen too—to prove how great and generous he was as a king.

When Samuel heard this, he cried all night to the Lord. The Lord answered, "I am grieved that I have made Saul king, because he has turned away from me and has not carried out my instructions" (1 Samuel 15:11). So Samuel confronted Saul about his disobedience.

Instead of considering his wrong, Saul started making excuses: "Come on, Samuel, it's not such a big deal. We just kept a few sheep and oxen—they're the best livestock we could find, and we were going to use them as an offering to God!"

The Lord, however, sees the sin deep in the heart. He isn't impressed by excuses. He wants obedience.

He expects us to take responsibility for our sin and leave the sins of other people to him. Sure, many of us have hurts and scars from the past, but God can heal those hurts and give us a new start. He longs to renew us from within. He can't do that, though, unless we stop making excuses and start taking responsibility for our actions. The only thing he accepts for sin is repentance because repentance separates us from the sin that kills us spiritually!

You see, there won't be a third option for Judgment Day. It's not going to be yes, no, or best excuse. It's going to be "yes, I did that" or "no, I didn't"—either "yes, I repented of my sin" or "no, I didn't." That's God's standard. Don't find out the hard way, like Saul did, that God doesn't tolerate excuses.

Saul was told by Samuel, "Because you have rejected the word of the Lord, he has rejected you as king," and later the Lord did raise up David as king. Saul's life ended in defeat.

Where do we get the idea that we won't end up the same way or that God will accept our excuses for our sin?

True, making excuses for sin seems the easiest, most natural thing to do. Instead of recognizing God at work, it's easy to make excuses for the wrongs we do: "Well, I'm not so bad" or "I try to live a good life" or "I get it right 90 percent of the time." Then there is the great excuse of our time, the one you see on bumper stickers everywhere: "Christians aren't perfect, just forgiven."

Sure, Christians are forgiven. But if that's where we've stopped, then we've short-changed God because he wants to make us perfect so we can be light to the world. He wants to make us more than just forgiven. He wants to make us holy.

20

THE PROMISE FOR
DEHYDRATED SOULS

Some Christians wonder why they continue to live in pain, confusion, or with no sense of direction. Some even blame it on God. But God wants to make us clean so He can pour his living water through us—rivers of it like he promised!

Maybe no one told us that accepting the Lord means rejecting sin, an often dirty or painful process.

Think about it. If you want a glass of water to drink what's the first thing you do? Make sure the glass is clean! If you pour clean water into a dirty glass, the water loses its purity. It's no longer fit to drink.

It's the same with the Holy Spirit. The Spirit can't be poured into this world through an unclean vessel, yet we are taught to clean up our behavior and the emphasis is placed on outer appearance, the part of us that others see. So we do our best to look all bright and shiny on the outside with everything holding together. Meanwhile our insides can be full of crud.

The Holy Spirit sees right through that because he looks on the heart, where he's going to dwell. It's as if he comes and inspects the premises. He wants to see if we've cleaned up so he can move in. If we haven't, he gets on our case. He tries to get our attention. He brings conviction.

If we continually ignore him or try to push him away with excuses, we'll keep heading into darkness, all the while blaming God for not rescuing us! But if we acknowledge the Spirit, then he will work within us to clean up our hearts. If we repent of our sin and make some deliberate decisions to live differently, he will forgive us our sins. He'll move in to take up residence in our new hearts. Once he's residing there, he gives us the power we need to live a godly life.

Here's the big challenge: Sometimes we have to clean up things we don't want to. There's a battle of wills going on—God's will or ours. We may have some sins that are painful to face. Some require us to make restitution for something we've stolen or make us ask forgiveness from someone we've wronged. Life may suddenly seem dark and stormy, but look at this promise:

> For His anger lasts only a moment, but His favor lasts a lifetime; weeping may remain for a night, but rejoicing comes in the morning.
> —PSALM 30:5

Joy comes in the morning, along with peace and other fruit of the Spirit. All of it comes as a result of a repentant heart and a righteous lifestyle. Fruit doesn't come from nowhere. You don't plant an apple seed one day and pick apples the next. You've got to cultivate, water, fertilize, and prune. If the process is done right, you get some fruit. The fruit of the Spirit comes through the process of repentance. You cultivate your heart, plow it up, make it soft by repentance; the Holy Spirit waters, tends, and brings the fruit—a harvest of righteousness.

The pain is worth the process. The fruit of the Spirit will be our reward!

21

A NEW SPIN
ON FAMILY VALUES

When Melody and I first became Christians, we felt we'd been adopted into a huge new family. We met wonderful new grandparents, parents, and older brothers and sisters in the Lord. We never knew such a great family existed before we met the Lord, and we had no idea about Christian love, fellowship, and support. Then suddenly we were surrounded by these people who loved Jesus—and us!

We wanted to love them all right back! So whenever we met anyone even remotely interested in knowing Jesus, we introduced them to our new family. We wanted them to see the reality of Christ at work in the lives of all these people. Because we were new Christians, we figured older Christians could answer all the questions and radiate Christ at the same time.

Then we went over to Leo's house.

We'd hoped that day to find our Christian friends, so they could talk with a young woman we'd met and help answer some of her questions about the Lord. We were told our friends were at Leo's.

What a sad surprise when we walked in and found a party in full swing. People were lying around, tripping out on drugs, and guzzling beer.

One guy even jumped into the pool—nude! We recognized some people from our Bible study. Our hearts hit the floor. Here were people we respected obviously in no condition to witness to anyone.

Melody and I walked out, stunned, and the young woman with us was disillusioned. Our idealistic little world was shattered.

Man, were we confused. Did we really know these people after all? It was like they had two lives. One life they wore at Bible studies like a suit of clothes—a church suit; and another life they wore for their secular friends—a pagan suit.

Since then I've seen many Christians who are on fire for the Lord one minute, but cool off fast when unsaved friends are around. That's not being on fire. That's just playing with fire.

Jesus said it plainly—"the man who loves his life will lose it, while the man who hates his life in this world will keep it for eternal life" (John 12:25). When you become a Christian you don't just get a new family—you get a new life.

22

WHAT HAPPENS WHEN GOD GETS UNDER YOUR SKIN?

Hundreds of people have come up to me after concerts and asked for counsel, prayer, and help. They don't like it when I point out that no one can help them unless they're willing to stop living a double life—they must choose a life of either following sin or following Jesus.

Likewise, I've pleaded with Christian music artists who have live-in girlfriends, with "Spirit-filled" Christians who won't give up getting drunk, with friends who get a high from Jesus on Sunday and a high from drugs on Monday. These are people who know the Word of God and represent that Word to others. But they trade on the grace of God, hoping he will wait for them to get their act together.

Unless they see the deeper truth, though, they're headed for a big crash. Paul knew what to do with the old man inside each of us—that old life that tries to kill God's Spirit in us. Paul told the Romans, "In the same way, count yourselves dead to sin but alive to God in Christ Jesus" (Romans 6:11), or as the King James Version puts it, "Reckon ye also yourselves to be dead indeed unto sin."

What does it mean to "count" or "reckon" yourself dead to sin?

The word "reckon" means to "calculate, compute, regard, consider with confidence, rely, count, or base your plans upon." So Paul is saying don't plan on sinning any more. Think of yourselves as being dead to sin. That means don't snort cocaine. Stop lying. Quit going out with the men or women who tempt you into bed. Don't steal anymore. You're dead to all that sin. It's over. It's no longer a choice for you so don't even toy with it.

Does this mean it's impossible for people with Christ in them to sin?

No, we don't become robots when we accept Christ. Each of us continues to be very capable of sinning. But when we reckon ourselves dead to sin, we recognize that sin is no longer our master. We are no longer compelled to sin, no longer held hostage by it. There is a way out because Jesus has become our new master and Lord. We have to look at our behavior and say, "This is spiritual death." We don't say: "Well, I guess it's not so good. Maybe I should stop...sometime...when it's not fun anymore or hurts someone."

No. We choose a new path. We base our plans upon the belief that we, meaning the old self inside, are dead to sin. We stop choosing sin and instead make choices that lead to life.

23

THE DECIDING PLACE

Every day we're presented with choices. For example, God tells us to serve. So we start doing what God has told us to do: at home, at work, in ministry. About this time our flesh sneaks up and says, "I'm so disappointed. Nobody knows how hard I'm working. Nobody appreciates what I'm doing. Nobody cares about me at all. People just like me for what I can do. I'm being used."

Sometimes Satan gets in on the act, too. He comes to us as a whiny little voice in our minds and starts planting sorry thoughts there. Every one of his negative thoughts is like an arrow that shoots us down from what God clearly has told us to do.

Here's the place where we can decide to give life to our old, self-centered flesh or put it to death so we can walk in our new, God-centered spiritual lives. We can say, "I agree with what my flesh is telling me. These people probably are using me." So we can bring that thought to the front of our minds, entertain it, act on it—and when we do, we enter into sin. Or we can say, "I serve God, not other men. God is building something into my life through serving, even when no one notices, because 'it is more blessed to give than to receive'" (Acts 20:35).

See? We do have a choice in reckoning ourselves dead to sin. That's what Paul meant in Romans 6:4, where he talks about dying with Jesus. Spiritually, death with Christ is imputed to us once and for all at salvation. Practically, we have to live it out daily in our lives.

Paul said he had to die daily (1 Corinthians 15:31). So do you. Every day you will come to a crossroad: Do you choose life in Christ or sin and death?

24

STRENGTH FOR
THE TUG OF WAR

Do you ever feel like on one side you have God urging you to make righteous choices, and on the other side you have your flesh, the devil, the world, your old friends, and the media urging you to make wrong choices?

It's a giant tug of war, and the tension can leave you feeling worse than before you became a Christian!

That tension is real. It's as if there are two teams living within your one body: the flesh and the Holy Spirit. But there is no common ground between the flesh and the Spirit—not in my life, nor in yours. This leaves us with a dilemma, and Paul talked a lot about this struggle. In his letter to the Galatians he listed the goals of the two teams that war within.

> For the sinful nature desires what is contrary to the Spirit, and the Spirit what is contrary to the sinful nature. They are in conflict with each other, so that you do not do what you want. But if you are led by the Spirit, you are not under law. The acts of the sinful nature are obvious: sexual immorality, impurity and debauchery; idolatry and witchcraft; hatred, discord, jealousy, fits of rage, selfish ambition, orgies, and the like. I

warn you, as I did before, that those who live like this will not inherit the kingdom of God. But the fruit of the Spirit is love, joy, peace, patience, kindness, goodness, faithfulness, gentleness, and self control. Against such things there is no law.

—GALATIANS 5:17-23

I've surely experienced this. Every day I've done a hundred things I didn't want to do: reacted negatively to people, given in to bad attitudes, used a sarcastic tone of voice. So the things I didn't want to do, I did; the things I've wanted to do I seem unable to accomplish. Paul said this drove him crazy, too:

So I find this law at work: When I want to do good, evil is right there with me. For in my inner being I delight in God's law; but see another law at work in the members of my body, waging war against the law of my mind and making me a prisoner of the law of sin at work within my members. What a wretched man I am! Who will rescue me from this body of death?

—ROMANS 7:21-24

You can feel Paul getting weary in the battle: losing strength and wanting to lie down and give up. Where does the strength come from to win? Paul answered his own question: "Thanks be to God— through Jesus Christ our Lord" (Romans 7:25)!

You can rest in that strength. Author Andrew Murray said, "Abide in Jesus, the—sinless one— which means give up all of self and its life, and dwell in God's will and rest in His strength. This is what brings the power that does not commit sin."

25

REAL WILLPOWER

The only way to ever subdue the flesh is when we allow Jesus victory and let God work in us. That means first making the right decision. That's our part because God created in us something given to no other creature: a will.

Take dogs, for example. When it's mating time a dog goes out and finds a partner. They mate and have puppies. The female dog doesn't think: *I wonder what kind of a dad he'll make?* or *Is this the color coat I want for my puppies?* No, dogs were made simply to do what instinct programs them to do.

We, on the other hand, have choices to make. God has given us the choice of how to live our lives. Our will is the only thing in the universe God does not own. In this area, and this area only, he has allowed his creation to make decisions that affect him. Notice how many times in the Bible it's recorded that God felt anger, disappointment, regret, and sorrow—all because he gave people the choice of how to live.

Yet God won't take control of our wills by force. If we want him to have control of our lives, we must give that control to him. If we choose to go it alone, we're doomed to failure. We need God's help. But when we lay our lives and will upon God's altar, we free God to be our partner. When we use our will to make godly choices, turn our whole hearts toward him, and step out in faith, he moves heaven and earth to see that we have victory over the flesh. Then nothing is impossible.

26

There's No Place Like Home

In our first few years in California the Lord sent two girls to live with us. Both girls had been involved in drugs and prostitution. Although they weren't tempted to run off and become prostitutes again, the freewheeling life of drugs, wild parties, and breaking all the rules was often difficult for them to resist. On more than one occasion we had to lay down the law, and they had some setbacks—and choices to make.

Their story is like the one of the prodigal son that Jesus told in Luke 15. There was only one thing the father would not do for his son. He would not send his servant out to find the son and drag him home. The father knew he had to let his son make his own choice.

Meanwhile the son had to recognize where his lifestyle was leading—to a pigsty and death! He had to humble himself and turn his face toward home. Once the son made that choice to return to the law of his father's house, and he got within sight of home, an uproar began. The father rushed out in welcome, gave his son a robe and a ring, and threw a big homecoming party.

God is the same with us. We have a war going on within, a war between our flesh and the Spirit of God. It's our choice which side we will throw the weight of our will into. If we want to pull for the side of sin and death we can do that. But we also have the Spirit of Christ within, bringing life, hope, and righteousness in our bodies. Like the prodigal son's father, Christ waits eagerly to give us power and authority—the power and authority we need to stand against temptation. God's only condition is that we make the choice to turn from temptation. As Paul told the Philippians, we must reckon ourselves dead to our own desires:

> What is more, I consider everything a loss compared to the surpassing greatness of knowing Christ Jesus my Lord, for whose sake I have lost all things. I consider them rubbish that I may gain Christ and be found in him, not having a righteousness that comes from the law, but that which is through faith in Christ—the righteousness that comes from God and is by faith.
>
> —PHILIPPIANS 3:8-10

As Paul, the prodigal son, and those two girls who lived with us discovered making the right choices, bit by bit, allows God to transform our lives. Consistently over the years the two young women who lived with us yielded their wills to the Lord; if you met them today you would never guess their backgrounds.

That's living in the power of the resurrection, a power that's at your disposal if you set your heart to follow Christ—if you make your heart his home.

27

JUICE YOUR SPIRIT

When Paul talks in Ephesians 1:18-19 about the resurrection power of Jesus, he's talking about the ultimate power source. That power source is available to everyone!

When we make a conscious choice to obey the Spirit of God within us, and resist our flesh, the power switch is turned on.

Then we begin to see the truth of Paul's promise: "I have been crucified with Christ and I no longer live, but Christ lives in me" (Galatians 2:20). Or, as Paul told the Romans: "Now if we died with Christ, we believe that we will also live with him....The death he died, he died to sin once for all; but the life he lives, he lives to God" (Romans 6:8,10).

It's the power of God that's released in us, and he gives us that power to live righteously.

If you have never done this before, do it now: Consider yourself dead to sin and alive to Christ. Constantly, daily, go before God and ask: "Please awaken the new me. Bury the old me in a grave. I don't want to have any more to do with the old me." You'll see how the eternal power of God, made available by the finished work of the cross, will help you walk in resurrection life.

28

GRACE FOR THE GRIND

Do you know another word for the power that comes when you reckon yourself dead to sin?

It's "grace," that infinite, patient strength of God working in the human spirit. Grace is what sets you apart from the world as a believer. People who aren't Christians can read the Bible to find out what God requires, but they can never do what God wants in their own strength. They don't have the grace of God within them. But when you have Christ in you, Paul said you stand in grace:

> Therefore, since we have been justified through faith, we have peace with God through our Lord Jesus Christ, through whom we have gained access by faith into this grace in which we now stand. And we rejoice in the hope of the glory of God.
>
> —ROMANS 5:1-2

It's as though you really are standing in the powerful currents of an ocean. Grace surrounds you, moves you; in every way you look, there is grace.

It is all-important that you rely on the power and grace of God so you can live your life day after day without burning out. In fact, it's impossible to live out the gospel in your own strength.

You see, grace is like oil in the engine. When Henry Ford put his first engine together he probably looked at all the pieces of metal and said to himself, "How am I going to keep this thing from grinding itself into dust in two hours?"

Someone said, "Oil."

In a similar way we go to God and ask: "How am I going to live this life? How am I going to overcome the opposite impulses going on inside me? How do I keep these forces from grinding me down?"

God, so patient, so full of grace, says, "The oil of the Spirit, the Spirit of grace, will keep you from burning up and grinding to a halt."

When Christ lives within you, He gives you the power to choose righteousness. God reaches down in grace and takes your hand; together there is no sin or temptation you cannot conquer.

29

KEEP YOUR EYE ON THAT GUY

You'll never beat the devil by ignoring him. That's not how Jesus found victory over Satan. No, when you decide to be a disciple of Jesus, you can expect the same treatment from Satan that Jesus got.

So was Jesus really "tempted in every way, just as we are—yet was without sin," as Hebrews 4:15 says?

That's what Luke 4:1-13 shows. After his baptism, Jesus was led by the Spirit out into the wilderness, where he fasted and prayed for 40 days. At the end, when he was very weak, the devil came to him. Now the devil didn't just use one temptation, but three different strategies to try and seduce Jesus.

The first played on Jesus' need for physical sustenance. Satan told Jesus, "If you are the Son of God, tell this stone to become bread" (Luke 4:3). Notice how the word "if" is an attempt to goad Jesus into proving he is the Son of God, a fact Satan already knew well!

The second temptation, where the devil showed Jesus all the kingdoms of the world in a single moment, offered a quick way for Jesus to "own" the earth. The devil said: "I will give you all their authority and splendor, for it has been given to me, and I can give it to anyone I want to. So if you worship me, it will all be yours" (Luke 4:6-7). This time Satan offered Jesus the cheap, easy way out, a way to get what he wanted—us—without all the fuss, bother, agony, and blood of the crucifixion.

The third temptation was an attempt to get Jesus to tempt God himself. The devil took Jesus to the pinnacle of the temple in Jerusalem, and said:

> If you are the Son of God...throw yourself down from here. For it is written: "He will command his angels concerning you to guard you carefully; they will lift you up in their hands, so that you will not strike your foot against a stone."
>
> —LUKE 4:9-10

Each time Jesus resisted the devil until Satan gave up and withdrew. Even in a weakened physical state, Jesus' heart was found to be pure. You'd think Satan would have quit. No way.

Luke 4:13 says: "When the devil had finished all this tempting, he left [Jesus] until an opportune time."

Look at that statement again—"until an opportune time." Obviously the devil was not going to let the whole matter drop! He was going to keep an eye on things, waiting to see if there was a moment when Jesus would let down his guard. Maybe there would be one moment when Jesus' flesh might be exposed; if ever that occurred, Satan was ready to pounce.

Scripture shows that even for Jesus, temptation wasn't a onetime battle. You know, resist once and it's over. Resisting the devil isn't a onetime thing for any of us. Satan is always on the lookout for an opportune time to get at us. He might wait until, like Jesus, we are at a low point physically, or he might wait until we've reached some spiritual milestone so he can lure us into pride and independence.

Being aware of Satan's tactics and ready to resist him every day is half the battle. Jesus said, "Watch and pray so that you will not fall into temptation. The spirit is willing, but the body is weak" (Mark 14:38).

30

IF IT WALKS LIKE A DUCK, IT STILL COULD BE A QUACK

What would be the most opportune time for Satan to tempt you away from serving God? How about when your heart is not focused on being with Jesus! The biggest mistake Christians can make is to think we have the power to resist the devil when we're out of relationship with Jesus. If we're not in Christ, if we're not walking by the Spirit, we're sitting ducks.

That's what seven brothers discovered in apostle Paul's day. When Paul was in Ephesus, miracles were happening: people were healed and demons were cast out of tormented souls. These seven brothers, young guys, watched all of this and were amazed. They decided that if Paul could do it, so could they. They memorized what Paul said and looked for someone to try it out on. Along came a demon-possessed man, and they began casting the evil spirit out of him in Jesus' name. Big mistake! Luke tells us:

> Some Jews who went around driving out evil spirits tried to invoke the name of the Lord Jesus over those who were demon-possessed. They would say, "In the name of Jesus, who Paul preaches, I

command you to come out." Seven sons of Sceva, a Jewish chief priest, were doing this. One day, the evil spirit answered them, "Jesus, I know, and I know Paul, but who are you?" Then the man who had the evil spirit jumped on them and overpowered them all. He gave them such a beating that they ran out of the house naked and bleeding.

—Acts 19:13-16

What a rude awakening for these seven guys! Think about it. The odds were seven-to-one in favor of the brothers. Even in the flesh they should have been able to take on one man. But the demon tore off their clothes, then beat them to bloody pulps.

They must have asked themselves, "How did this happen? Didn't we do everything Paul did?"

Yes, they did. But they were not everything that Paul was—Paul was a disciple of Jesus. The seven sons of Sceva were impostors. The demon could tell in a second that they had no real authority. They were just using the name of Jesus for their own ends, without any understanding or concern for the kingdom of God. So while the brothers had the right actions, and even acted in Jesus' name, they had the wrong heart.

You can take to heart Jesus' promise to his disciples: You will have the power in his name to resist the devil, when you believe in the Lord and are baptized and saved (Mark 16:17).

31

DOUBLE AGENTS FOR
THE GREAT RESISTANCE

In the war with temptation, what's the best way to resist the devil? The Bible shows two.

The first is to set your heart on knowing Christ because the closer you are to Jesus, the less vulnerable you are to Satan. Even in the Old Testament you see this principle at work. In times of attack, if you don't have a relationship with Jesus, you are like the seven sons of Sceva (Acts 19:13-16), left to wonder why the enemy leaves you beaten and battered every time. But if you are righteous, you can run for cover in your relationship with the Lord, trusting in his Spirit. Proverbs 18:10 says, "The name of the LORD is a strong tower; the righteous run to it and are safe."

The second way of resistance is to know the devil's tactics. Peter said: "Be self-controlled and alert. Your enemy the devil prowls around like a roaring lion looking for someone to devour" (1 Peter 5:8).

When Peter describes Satan prowling like a lion, you can see the pattern of deceit the devil uses—he's a scavenger! He feeds on wounded and vulnerable people, anyone who has strayed from the safe sheepfold because some area of his or her life is not fully submitted to Christ.

Maybe it starts with a little bitterness stored up in the heart. Maybe there's a little wounded pride or arrogance. Maybe some think they can ignore wise counsel. Once you're separated in spirit from the fellowship and protection of Christ and other Christians, that's when Satan goes on the prowl.

To try and tempt Jesus, the devil waited until the Lord was physically weak in the wilderness. The devil looks for your moment of weakness or for you to wander into the wilderness. The good thing, as Proverb 18:10 says, is that in the war with sin the Lord provides a strong refuge—himself.

32

WALK RIGHT THIS WAY

A lot of Christians toy with temptation. They never put much distance between themselves and the things that pull them into sin, and they don't seem to see sin as serious. But playing games with sin can destroy our lives, spiritually and physically.

See, sin works like sexually transmitted diseases (STDs). I know this isn't the most delicate of examples, but it's accurate. A person gets STDs from having so-called "fun." The first signs are difficult to detect and almost painless. Then STDs take root in the body and, if left untreated, some can eventually blind their hosts and drives people crazy—crazy to death! Yes, STDs kill.

So does sin. It seems fun, but it's sinister, like swallowing a sugar-coated, time-release capsule of cyanide. A little bit of compromise here, a little bit there, and you don't see how it's all piling up in your life. But it's there, all right, and it's deadly.

So sin creeps into your life in all sorts of ways. Maybe you feel bored with your spiritual life or angry at a brother. You begin to think all this Christianity stuff is a waste of time; secretly, you think no one knows. If you have problems with lust or sexual immorality, you might begin to hang around adult bookstores. Oh sure, you just look and don't buy, right? Or if you've been into alcohol, you pick up some white wine—an expensive bottle because, after all, you're no wino, right?

What happens is you've moved in your spirit from commitment to messing again with sin. You're just seeing how close you can come to the fire without being burned. Twice Paul warned Timothy against this:

> But you, man of God, flee from all this, and pursue righteousness, godliness, faith, love, endurance and gentleness.
>
> —1 TIMOTHY 6:11

> Flee the evil desires of youth, and pursue righteousness, faith, love and peace, along with those who call on the Lord out of a pure heart.
>
> —2 TIMOTHY 2:22

That's right: Flee. Run. Get as far and fast as you can from everything that gives Satan a claw-hold on your life. But where to run? Chase after righteousness, godliness, gentleness, faith, and love—all the things you'll find in the Lord.

See, it comes back to pursuing God, seeking him daily and giving yourself to him. As Paul said in Ephesus (Ephesians 4:27), running away from the temptations that you once would have toyed with keeps you from getting tripped up in Satan's footholds.

33

SURVIVAL STORIES BEGIN
WITH THIS

In the apostle Paul's day, soldiers had to wear a lot of armor: a helmet, breastplate, shoes, shield. Leaving off even one piece, like the breastplate, made them vulnerable, practically begging to be shot in the heart with an arrow.

It's the same for our spirits. Paul told the Ephesians who were surrounded by pagan idol-worship and sick lifestyles: "Put on the full armor of God so that you can take your stand against the devil's schemes" (Ephesians 6:11).

First, protect your very core by buckling on the belt of Truth (Ephesians 6:14). That means read God's Word, learn it, memorize it, and have it ready when Satan attacks. That's what Jesus did. Remember when, after his 40-day fast, he was tempted by the devil to turn stones into bread (Luke 4:3)? Jesus responded by quoting Deuteronomy 8:3: "...Man does not live on bread alone but on every word that comes from the mouth of the Lord." Can't you just see Satan knocked back a few steps! The Truth drove him off; he knew he couldn't penetrate Jesus' spiritual armor that way.

So the devil looks for another way to tempt. He'll sneak up and aim to pierce your heart, saying,

"Look at you—you've blown it again. You're never going to get it right, are you?"

That's where the breastplate of righteousness comes in (Ephesians 6:14). It's not your own goodness that protects your heart, but God's righteousness that allows you to say what you know deep down, "I am growing in Christ slowly, every day, and there is no condemnation because I'm in Christ Jesus."

So Satan looks for another way to trip you up—literally. That's why Paul says make sure your "feet are fitted with the readiness that comes from the gospel of peace" (Ephesians 4:15).

That's just what Robert, a new believer, did. His high school physical education coach announced that the class was required to jump high hurdles the next week. Robert was not only unathletic, but also overweight. He expected to trip, land face-first on the track, and give the whole class one more chance to laugh at him.

Some other guys feared the same fate, so they forged excuses from their parents to cut class. Robert wanted to save himself the pain and embarrassment too, but he knew lying wasn't right. He jumped the hurdles and didn't do too badly—just one or two falls, no broken bones, and nobody laughing at him.

A couple weeks later a classmate confronted Robert, "You stuck it out even though you knew you were going to bite the dust. Why?"

Robert saw his chance to talk about how he was tempted to skip the hurdles too, but lying would have dashed the integrity of his relationship with Jesus. The classmate knew Robert really believed what he said—and God used Robert's readiness to be a witness for Jesus and to get into another young man's heart. Robert's classmate got saved that day!

Can't you see Satan fume by now and hurl flaming arrows? But as they come in screaming, Paul says you can swing your shield of faith (Ephesians 4:16). Your trust in God actually extinguishes those flaming arrows! See, God's shield is not something you hide behind. It's something you aggressively wield with unshakable certainty that God is who he says he is and that he's done for everyone what he said he'd do.

Of course that's when the devil goes for the head. Satan knows that whoever controls the mind controls the body. To stand against his attack, Paul says you need the helmet of salvation and sword of the Spirit (Ephesians 4:17). As you surrender to God every new day, he cleanses your mind. He renews it, taking away the junk and old thought-patterns. When you get your head straight about God, and really believe his Word, then that Word becomes your sword for attacking.

Is your sword sharpened for the attack? Do you have the Word of God stored in your heart, ready to protect yourself and witness to all Jesus has done for you? When you put on the full armor of God you are like the smart soldier, the one who lives to tell about the battle.

34

A Prayer for the Pretenders

You know, our lives can seem so nice and spiritual on the outside, but on the inside usually things aren't pretty. We're a mess. We try to hide sin and wickedness. The truth is, we all fake it some of the time and some Christians fake it a lot of the time. But eventually we can't fake it anymore. We can't hold things together. The pressure gets too great and out comes the true state of our hearts. Maybe we've been pretending to be spiritual and patient with someone, and one day out bursts all our criticalness and anger.

It doesn't have to be that way. We don't have to fake it. We can choose to do as John tells us: walk in the light—live honestly with God, letting him show us the truth about ourselves and our hidden motives. John said, "But if we walk in the light, as he is in the light, we have fellowship with one another, and the blood of Jesus, his Son, purifies us from all sin" (1 John 1:7). That means daily letting others see the weak state of our hearts too. It's humbling to allow others to see our weaknesses. But we do it so they can encourage us, support us, and hold us accountable in certain areas.

Not only that, we can bring things into the light and ask God to forgive us of our sin (and sin is always at the root, isn't it?). The promise is sure. John says, "If we confess our sins, [God] is faithful and just and will forgive us our sins and purify us from all unrighteousness" (1 John 1:9).

That's a huge weapon against temptation. Another is prayer. Paul says: "And pray in the Spirit on all occasions with all kinds of prayers and requests. With this in mind, be alert and always keep on praying for all the saints" (Ephesians 6:18).

So prayer is our ultimate weapon. But we can be so foolish when we're attacked by the devil—prayer is the first thing we let drop. We run around to all our friends and whine, "Oh, I'm under attack. Lay hands on me! Pray for me!" When we're attacked we should stand our ground and pray more—and more fervently.

Sure, it's good to ask our brothers and sisters for their prayer support, but we can't depend solely on the prayers of others to grow strong. Prayer is the lifeline that keeps us connected to God. If our lifelines are cut, the devil's victory is inevitable. But if we stay plugged into God, who is our life, then we'll always win over our adversary the devil.

Do you see the whole thing now? With our sin forgiven, and with others surrounding us and holding us accountable, there's not much left for the devil to get a hold of is there? There's nothing we're hiding in dark corners that we don't want others to see: No secret sin buried away, no weak flesh exposed for the prowling lion to jump on, no pretend spirituality!

35

THE WAY TO WIN:
GIVE IN!

I meet Christians all the time who are more like the seven sons of Sceva (Acts 19:13-16) than true disciples. They've been beaten up by the devil so they're offended at God. The real problem is they aren't honest with themselves. They refuse to run very fast away from their sin; they don't take the time to know God's Word and arm themselves spiritually—and forget about regular prayer!

These pseudo-Christians continue to live in pride, pretending they're doing fine spiritually, when really they're hiding secret sins. The problem is that they're still living self-centered lives at the core. All this resistance to God! Then they wonder why they're living defeated lives.

It doesn't make much sense, does it?

Well, we can spout all the Scriptures we want about our spiritual birthright, our total victory over Satan, but that total victory hasn't come yet. There's a spiritual war to be fought! Disciples of Jesus must be on the front lines! We must go to war for the sake of other people who will die and go to hell if we don't win them for Christ. And we must stop looking simply for God's comfort and blessing. Instead we need to get out there where lost people are being cut down by Satan.

That means we must submit to God, who wants us to get free. Yes, James 4:7—"Resist the devil, and he will flee"—is true. We have a spiritual birthright to victory when we follow Christ. But look at the key to claiming that birthright, the first part of the Scripture: "Submit yourselves, then, to God...." In the war against Satan's hold on us or others, submitting comes first! Total submission to God is what's going to win the war.

36

WHO'S THE BOSS?

Zeal for God is a good thing, right? Do you remember how Jesus reacted when he stepped into the great tabernacle at Jerusalem, where he'd gone to celebrate Passover? John, one of his friends and followers gives this account:

> In the temple courts [Jesus] found men selling cattle, sheep and doves, and others sitting at tables, exchanging money. So he made a whip out of cords, and drove all from the temple area, both sheep and cattle; he scattered the coins of the money changers and overturned their tables. To those who sold doves he said, "Get these out of here! How dare you turn my Father's house into a market!"
>
> —JOHN 2:14-17

Imagine how the disciples felt watching their master upset the lovely decorum of the temple: the noise, the dust, the shouting, the money spilling, the tables upturned! The disciples probably were shocked at first (how dare Jesus do such a thing!). But then they were elated. We know when it was over they reminded one another of the Scripture that says, "For zeal for your house consumes me..." (Psalm 69:9). They must have thought, *Now we see what that means. Jesus loves his father's house so deeply that he won't tolerate sin in it!*

That's how I would have felt. "Good job, Jesus! Show everyone who's the boss!"

No doubt Jesus' actions that day excited everyone. The common people were thrilled to have a hero who could kick around all the religious windbags and money-grubbing scum; if it meant popularity or flexing their muscles, the disciples were all for it, too.

The only problem was no one understood one fundamental fact about human nature: Zeal, or earnestness and fervor for advancing a cause, is not necessarily a good thing—at least not our human zeal. See, that cause can be good or bad, focused or misguided. As we read through the Gospels, we see that the disciples' zeal often was misguided.

So was the Pharisees'. No one could say these guys didn't have zeal! Everything they did involved religious duties and doctrines, but their passion was founded on legalism and not on knowing God. The Pharisees promoted a cause that was cold and lifeless, a cause that made their hearts proud and arrogant.

We love to poke fun at that and read the rebukes Jesus used to level those Pharisees, but we're just as capable of misdirecting our zeal to useless religious activities, things that are all for outward show, stuff that generates heat but not light.

That's how I was when I first became a Christian. I had lots of zeal. I never gave too much thought about where my energy was directed, and I did things that were pointless, ungodly, and unproductive. I've probably not been alone.

We all can misdirect our energy at times. Like the Pharisees, we get trapped by our own zealousness. Sometimes we fight causes that aren't God's. Other times we judge others, or we argue over the Bible. Too often we seek blessings more than the giver of those blessings. Each of these acts of zeal wreak havoc and destroy the body of Christ—and none of these things constitutes true zeal for God.

You can replace your relationship with the Lord with your righteous activity, but you can't earn your salvation by proving how zealous you are. The trick is to look at what advances your relationship with the Lord or the kingdom of God here on earth.

37

GIVE HIM YOUR EARS

You can be zealous for God, yet totally miss his big picture. Look at all the religious wars that have been fought, crusades that have been carried out—all the blood and destruction. How could zeal be so misdirected? How could people think they were committing such atrocities in the name of God? So much harm has been done to God's kingdom by so-called spiritual battles waged in the flesh!

Well, before standing in judgment of anyone else, we'd better realize we're all capable of pushing our own agenda ahead of God's agenda. Peter, who seemed to be the most ardent of the 12 disciples, learned this.

Wherever there was trouble, Peter was ready to jump in and save the day—at least in the flesh. Remember what he did in the the Garden of Gethsemane? It's the perfect example of misplaced zeal. As the soldiers came to take away Jesus, Peter pulled out his sword and cut off the ear of the high priest's servant. Jesus told Peter: "Put your sword back in its place...for all who draw the sword will die by the sword" (Matthew 26:52).

What did Peter think he was doing?

The same thing many of us think we're doing—protecting the Lord's reputation with ungodly methods, and hurting innocent people in the process. We forget God doesn't need or ask for our protection. Remember what else Jesus told Peter in the garden: "Do you think I cannot call on my Father, and he will at once put at my disposal more than twelve legions of angels?" (Matthew 26:53).

Peter, like the other disciples, totally missed God's big picture—his plan to send Jesus to the cross. Instead Peter had another plan. He still hoped Jesus would be the conquering hero. Peter had a lot of zeal for that, but he lacked the same passion when it came to being a spiritual companion to his Lord. Peter, who was so courageous about swinging his sword in public, was the same guy who abandoned Jesus at the moment the Lord took on his most difficult spiritual mission—humbling himself and going to the cross.

How is it that we're like that, so zealous to put on outward, heroic shows of loyalty for the faith and yet so reluctant to set aside our own agendas and do what Jesus wants?

Our zeal is misdirected. Paul reminds us, "The sinful mind is hostile to God. It does not submit to God's law, nor can it do so. Those controlled by the sinful nature cannot please God" (Romans 8:7-8).

We need to transfer our zeal from outward things to inward spiritual things. We need to be less willing to cut off ears in Jesus' name and more willing to humble ourselves by going into our prayer closets alone with God to get his agenda for our lives.

38

WHY THE PEOPLE'S COURT
IS HOT

When I was a new Christian I opened up my
Bible, then set myself up as a judge. I'd go into ministries and get loud about their need for correction.
Worse, within six months of my conversion, I was
on-stage performing—and judging things publicly.
Thousands of people came to hear me, and I really
got into letting them know what I thought.

One day God grabbed me by the collar and showed
me that judgment comes out of spiritual immaturity. A
mature Christian will confront unrighteousness in a
godly way: pray, discern, love, and counsel. If need be,
the mature Christian will rebuke, but never in a crit-
ical, destructive spirit—and never publicly to shame
and punish.

Immature Christians can have a lot of zeal, but
little wisdom. They can put fire and noise into things
that harm rather than help the cause of Christ. I fell
into that trap, just like two of Jesus' zealous disciples,
James and John. Do you remember what happened to
them?

> And [Jesus] sent messengers on
> ahead, who went into a Samaritan vil-
> lage to get things ready for him; but the
> people there did not welcome him

because he was heading for Jerusalem. When the disciples James and John saw this, they asked, "Lord, do you want us to call fire down from heaven to destroy them?" But Jesus turned and rebuked them, and they went to another village.

—LUKE 9:52-55

Like me, I doubt James and John expected a rebuke. As far as they were concerned, here was a whole village of people who had rejected Jesus. These folks had blown their chance to welcome the Lord! They deserved to be fried! It was time for this village to see the power of God!

However, if Jesus had wanted to call down fire on that Samaritan village, he certainly could have done it without the help of the disciples. Jesus had to grab James and John by the collar because they had tried to usurp the Lord's authority. He had to let them know that when you judge others, you step into the place of God—and God alone is the judge of the motives of people's hearts.

Face it, you'll always notice inconsistencies and sin in the lives of others; there always seem to be people with lifelong preoccupations of sitting in judgment over every ministry, elder, pastor, and Bible-study leader. These people get busy bringing down the gavel of judgment hard and heavy. They say they're trying to bring correction, but like the fire they call down they only consume others and destroy.

How many times have you acted like these guys, like James and John, or me? How often do you become a judge, and bring down the gavel on someone who's "obviously" in the wrong?

As a disciple and someone who knows God's Word, I've come to see that my zeal must be directed at me first. I can observe inconsistencies and judge, or I can use them as a reminder to beware of the sin in my own life.

Now I'm choosing to take Paul's advice to heart: "Brothers, if someone is caught in a sin, you who are spiritual should restore him gently..." (Galatians 6:1). Paul knew the Lord's correction is meant to bring restoration in relationship to the Lord and in ministry, not fiery destruction.

Restoration, after all, is God's goal, and it takes time.

39

WINNING WORDS VS.
WRANGLING ONES

When I was a new Christian I spent many useless hours (weeks, even months!) wrangling over
words. I'd argue over anything and everything: Can a
Christian be possessed by demons? Do you have to
be sprinkled or immersed to be truly baptized?
Should you be baptized in the name of Jesus only or
in the name of the Father, the Son, and the Holy
Spirit?

In some ways I set myself up for this. After concerts people came up to me and said, "You know, I
don't agree with your position on this or that." I'd sit
at the edge of the stage, a crowd would gather, and
I'd throw out Scripture with the other person lob-
bing back different verses. We'd have a great time
with our "flesh" exposed for all to see. I loved it!

I didn't realize then that my arguing could damage
my listeners' spirits. That's right. Paul says, "Keep
reminding them of these things. Warn them before
God against quarreling about words; it is of no value,
and only ruins those who listen" (2 Timothy 2:14).

So while I was thinking I was a big shot, some
spiritual authority, really I was just a debator with a
big ego. I may have sharpened my human argumen-
tation skills, but certainly not a spiritual talent for

being quiet, listening, and praying. Worse, the result of my actions was actually destructive.

"Godless chatter...will spread like gangrene," Paul said (2 Timothy 2:16-17). In Paul's day, if you saw a big blue streak going up your arm or leg, you ran to the surgeon who cut off the infected limb. It was either that or death, and surgery then wasn't like now. There was no anesthetic other than getting drunk or having someone knock you out. That Paul would compare such a painful, severe condition to the effects of a dispute over words tells me something: There's a lot more at stake in Scripture debates than who's right or wrong. I'm talking about eternal souls. Paul explains:

> But avoid foolish controversies and genealogies and arguments and quarrels about the law, because these are unprofitable and useless. Warn a divisive person once, and then warn him a second time. After that, have nothing to do with him. You may be sure that such a man is warped and sinful; he is self-condemned.
>
> —TITUS 3:9-11

You see, a contentious spirit is not true zeal for God. Immature Christians may think they know all the right answers and that everyone has to see things their way, but that's warped thinking, sinful, and even self-condemning. Again Paul explains:

> And the Lord's servant must not quarrel; instead, he must be kind to everyone, able to teach, not resentful. Those who oppose him he must gently instruct, in the hope that God will grant them repentance leading them to a knowledge of the truth, and that they will come

to their senses and escape from the trap of
the devil, who has taken them captive to
do his will.
—2 TIMOTHY 2:24-26

To grow in Christ, Paul said, there's only one standard and one motive acceptable to God. Ruthlessly
evaluate your speech. Are you arguing or chattering,
like I did, over things that produce a lot of heat and
maybe look like zeal for the Lord, but it doesn't produce the light God really wants? Use this final tip
from Paul to tell the difference:

Do not let any unwholesome talk come
out of your mouths, but only what is
helpful for building others up according
to their needs, that it may benefit those
who listen.
—EPHESIANS 4:29

40

Doing Good for the Wrong Reasons

From New Testament times until today, there have been people who preach the gospel for wrong reasons. They're not following Jesus. They're building their own kingdoms and their own egos. Some people get involved in Christianity simply because it is a market for their merchandise, and they can make money. They don't care as much if people become Christians as they do about selling their books or records.

Some people start with sincere motives, but their appetite for money and fame overcomes them—so they continue doing seemingly good things, but for all the wrong reasons. They're just putting up a front. They've learned how to effectively fake all the right moves and the right language.

But God will not be mocked.

For instance, read the story beginning in Acts 8:9, about a man named Simon who practiced magic and sorcery. Everyone in Samaria was astonished by the things he could do, and people called him "the divine...Great Power." Then Philip came to town preaching the good news. A revival hit: People began getting saved and baptized. Even Simon was converted. He began following Philip and saw all the miracles that occurred.

When word got back to the other apostles in Jerusalem about what was happening in Samaria, Peter and John were sent to check out things. They discovered the new converts had not yet received the baptism of the Spirit, so they began laying on hands and praying for people. Simon, once "the divine" sorcerer, liked what he saw:

> When Simon saw that the Spirit was given at the laying on of the apostles' hands, he offered them money and said, "Give me also this ability so that everyone on whom I lay my hands may receive the Holy Spirit." Peter answered, "May your money perish with you, because you thought you could buy the gift of God with money."
>
> —Acts 8:18-20

Sure, Simon's idea was misguided, but didn't he give up his sorcery business to follow the gospel? Wasn't Peter a little harsh with him?

I don't think so because while Simon had zeal, his zeal was directed at self-promotion—not knowing and sharing the love of God. Simon was ready to do whatever it took to get the power he wanted.

Sound familiar? Didn't some of us come to the Lord with wrong, selfish motives? Didn't we come because we were sick of our lifestyles, or we couldn't find peace, or we needed healing, or our marriages were on the rocks?

That's why we always need to check our motives for doing something, even a good thing. God wants true disciples who move beyond selfish motives to a pure motive—the desire to know God himself and the reason he created us.

Simon never made that shift. Scripture says he truly believed in the gospel, but it appears that he never got beyond desiring power. He became interested in the gospel because of what the disciples had to offer—their "tricks" were better than his. Simon didn't like the idea of being upstaged by the apostles. He wanted to gain more influence than anyone else.

What is your motive for following the gospel?

41

ZEAL APPEAL

I've seen celebrities and stars who become Christians but never lay down their music on the altar. They have lots of zeal, but are they putting that into seeking God?

These new believers don't always take the time they need to answer that. Before they're ready, they're getting pushed into the spotlight by publishers and record companies who begin selling Christian versions of their famous songs.

Other people look on and say, "That celebrity has so much zeal for God," when really these bystanders are just using a star's misdirected enthusiasm to pursue personal interests.

Soon even celebrated folks hit a pothole. Often they fall away, saying: "Christianity is a joke. It doesn't work."

That's what Simon the sorcerer did in Acts 8. Simon, who was celebrated in Samaria, had plenty of zeal to pursue the miracles, signs, and wonders that he saw the apostles do. But Simon didn't seem to have much interest in pursuing God himself. In fact, to our knowledge, Simon never accepted the lifestyle of discipleship the whole time he followed Philip. Instead Simon had his eyes on the gifts of God, rather than on the God of the gifts.

Paul saw the same kind of misdirected zeal among the Jews. He said:

> For I can testify about them that they are zealous for God, but their zeal is not based on knowledge. Since they did not know the righteousness that comes from God and sought to establish their own, they did not submit to God's righteousness.
>
> —ROMANS 10:2-3

If Paul looked at your life, would he say the same thing about you? Would he say, "I've got to give you credit. You sure have a lot of zeal for God. You're doing many things in the name of the Lord. But you don't know his righteousness."

See, even when you are successful in the things of the Lord, you must be careful not to look at the fruit and think it proves you're right with God. Nothing can replace your personal relationship with him, not even the fruit produced from ministries.

C.S. Lewis put it this way: "Do not let your happiness depend on something you may lose...only [upon] the beloved who will never pass away."

So ask yourself this: Am I using my zeal to try to gain something from God? Or am I using my zeal as an expression of my gratitude to God for all that he's already done for me?

42

WILL YOU SIP, SPLASH, OR SOAK?

You can be zealous at keeping the rules or a fervent debater and defender of the truth. You can chase after the gifts of the Spirit and even aggressively fight fleshly battles. But none of this is true zeal for God.

What is zeal for God, then?

Jesus made it pretty clear—it's giving all your energy and enthusiasm to God's right cause. In one of those great debates over truth, Jesus said:

> The most important [commandment]...is this: "Hear, O Israel, the Lord our God, the Lord is one. Love the Lord our God with all your heart and with all your soul and with all your mind and with all your strength." The second is this: "Love your neighbor as yourself." There is no commandment greater than these.
>
> —MARK 12:29-31

So we are supposed to direct all our zeal into our relationship with the Lord—and then into our relationships with our neighbors. Makes sense, doesn't it? God can take care of a lot of other causes without us, but he can't make us love him with all our hearts. That's the work we must do—pursue him with all our heart, soul, and strength.

"As the deer pants for streams of water, so my soul pants for you, O God," wrote David, a man after God's own heart (Psalm 42:1-2). "My soul thirsts for God, for the living God."

Thirsting after God is a pretty good description of true zeal. God wants us to fix our eyes and all our senses on him. Do you have that kind of desperation, that holy fire within to know God?

What about that second cause that Jesus said we are to advance? Do you love your neighbor as yourself? Notice that Jesus never said, "Correct your neighbor, or debate with or judge your neighbor." Just love your neighbors. Serve them.

Paul put it this way: "[Jesus] gave himself for us to redeem us from all wickedness and to purify for himself a people that are his very own, eager to do what is good" (Titus 2:14).

This is where eagerness counts because God doesn't want to be just a casual acquaintance. He wants to be an intimate part of your life—alive and burning at the core of your being—and he wants that relationship with all your neighbors, too.

43

THE GIFT THAT KEEPS ON GIVING

Are you zealous for good deeds and ready and willing to serve others? Or do you tend to be self-involved?

Watch out! Nobody's flesh likes the idea of serving others. In fact, an attitude of servanthood runs against the ego. Maybe that's why God put so much importance on service. According to James 1:27, "Religion that God our Father accepts as pure and faultless is this: to look after orphans and widows in their distress and to keep oneself from being polluted by the world."

See, he commands us to serve others. Disciples of Christ have no option but to do what God has told us. Look at what Jesus told his disciples about being great in the kingdom of God:

> ...Whoever wants to become great among you must be your servant, and whoever wants to be first must be your slave—just as the Son of Man did not come to be served, but to serve, and to give His life as a ransom for many.
>
> —MATTHEW 20:26

I can hear what many of you are thinking: But we don't need to prove ourselves to God or anybody else. He's given us salvation as a gift.

You're right. Salvation is God's gift, but he needs us to turn on our zeal to make salvation real in every area of our lives. The zeal that pleases God is strength and talent directed toward serving others. He wants you to train yourself to eagerly serve others in love and compassion.

This is true passion for God—to know and love him with a deep and consuming love, and to serve others the same way we would serve Jesus. Anything else is an imitation.

44

WHAT THE TAX COLLECTOR GOT

Today we're so interested in comforting each other: "You just answered an altar call? Said a sinner's prayer? Great, you're in! Now just try to stay out of trouble, will you? Oh, don't be too radical either. You might disturb people."

Well, I'd rather preach the neat and sweet stuff, believe me. People call you controversial when you tell them the hard stuff. It's much more...comfortable...to be a comforter. But look at the example Jesus gave us.

Jesus had a habit of walking through the countryside, gathering crowds of people around Him, then saying things that were pretty disturbing.

Imagine that you've left everything to follow him—your fishing boat, your tax-collecting booth, your mom and dad's beach house on the Sea of Galilee—and then Jesus says, "Not everyone who says to me, 'Lord, Lord,' will enter the kingdom of heaven, but only he who does the will of my Father who is in heaven" (Matthew 7:21).

What!?

That must be what Matthew, who recorded Jesus' words, thought. Remember, Matthew was the guy Jesus called out of a lot of sin and darkness: greed, extorting money from his own countrymen, and who knows what else! Yet even Matthew knew it was important to emphasize this side of Jesus' teaching. Matthew got it: Some people will go before the judgment seat of God, convinced they're going to heaven when they're not. Matthew caught on that it's not enough to answer God's invitation into the feast of his kingdom (Matthew 22:1-14). It's not enough to do good Christian deeds or perform miracles in Jesus' name.

Matthew knew, like we must know, that God is after something deeper and stronger.

45

WHO'S COMING TO DINNER?
THE SLOPPY JOES?

Jesus spoke to them again in parables, saying: "The kingdom of heaven is like a king who prepared a wedding banquet for his son....But when the king came in to see the guests, he noticed a man there who was not wearing wedding clothes. 'Friend,' he asked, 'how did you get in here without wedding clothes?' The man was speechless. Then the king told his attendants, 'Tie him hand and foot, and throw him outside, into the darkness, where there will be weeping and gnashing of teeth.' For many are invited, but few are chosen."

—MATTHEW 22:1-2, 11-14

Why did Jesus relate stories like this that shook up His most devoted followers? I think about this a lot because sometimes I find myself getting sloppy about my faith. My Bible can get dusty. I can hear about someone in need and say, "Wow, that's rough...well, what's on TV tonight?" I can drive past whole neighborhoods and cities and not worry that most of the people there are in spiritual darkness. I think, "Well, I'm on my way to the beach, God. Surf's up, you know! Maybe you can get somebody else who's not busy to witness to people today."

I'm aware of how I confuse God's grace with his infinite tolerance. Grace is the fact that he sent an invitation to his son's wedding feast at all. Grace is the fact that he purchased all these white robes—with Jesus' blood!—and then hands them out to sinners. Grace is the fact that when Satan comes to devour us, God steps in and says, "Back off! This is one of my children. Keep your hands off my kids."

Brothers and sisters, what is your heart attitude toward all those incredible gifts? When God says, "My son gave his life so you could be invited to this wedding feast," how do you respond? Do you say, "Okay, he gave his life for me so I'll give my life back to him"?

Most of us tend to run around waving our wedding invitation in people's faces, saying, "Man, look at this! I'm going to the wedding, aren't you?" Then we act like the guy in Jesus' parable. We show up in old, crummy jeans. We hang out in the back of the hall, stuffing ourselves at the buffet table. We don't act like guests anymore—and that's the problem I'm getting at.

So much of our Christianity is based on wanting to feel good. "Come to Jesus because it's a better high than drugs!" "Come and be blessed!" "The party's on!" We get comfortable and sloppy.

But there's another side to God, a side we'll all have to face some day: God as righteous judge. Don't be lulled to sleep, thinking you can ignore God's commands because, after all, he knows what a rough life you had before you were a Christian.

Yes, God comforts, but he comforts us with his grace so that instead of being sloppy in our faith, we continue to grow strong spiritually to do his will on earth. So God is gentle, and at the same time he's a righteous judge. What will you answer when he asks, "What did you do with all the grace I poured out on you? Did you do my will?"

46

IT'S A PROMISE

We keep on our breakfast tables little plastic boxes of Promise Cards filled with reminders of all the neat, sweet things about God.

Yeah, they're all true—every single one.

God has invited us all to live with Him in eternity—the greatest spiritual wedding feast you can imagine. That invitation into God's family is offered freely to everyone. John 3:16, probably the most well-known verse in the Bible, tells us so: "For God so loved the world that he gave his one and only Son, that whoever believes in him shall not perish but have eternal life." But like the cavalier man in Jesus' parable (Matthew 22, see devotion 45), many people will come to the wedding in an insulting way. They'll call themselves "Christian" and mistake God's invitation for his complete approval. They'll confuse God's love and grace with his righteous judgment.

You see, having an invitation to eternal life is not enough. There's an RSVP on that invitation. You have to respond to it. You can't just wave the invitation in God's face and say, "God is merciful, so if I'm still disobedient, when I get there it won't matter."

According to Jesus that won't work. God will judge every person according to what he or she did with the free righteousness he offered. Do you think he'd pour out the blood of his only Son just to have us trample it? Some preachers do. They make the judgment seat of Christ sound like a giant charity give-away. But by their lives, true Christians let the Lord know they're serious about accepting God's invitation.

We love to quote God's invitation, don't we? After all, Jesus said it in John 3:16. But the word "believe" doesn't mean we go around saying, "I believe, I believe, praise God, I believe." Even the demons believe in God that way (see James 2:19). The Christian's belief has to be much stronger than that.

The Greek word Jesus used for "believe" is *pisteuo*, which means to adhere to, have faith in, commit to, and to prove what you think and value by the way you live.

That's how you accept Christ's invitation—by clothing yourself in a new way of living: changing your spiritual robe, taking off your old life, and put-ting on your new life.

The New Testament clearly outlines some things that become part of the new life in Christ. It's these things that show you've come into real heart-union with Christ. It's the proof you've come to the wed-ding for Him. Jesus was clear about the first point:

> Whoever acknowledges me before men, I will also acknowledge him before my Father in heaven. But whoever dis-owns me before men, I will disown him before my Father in heaven.
>
> —MATTHEW 10:32-33

Don't you see? Anyone who isn't comfortable standing up for Christ here on earth will be very uncomfortable at the judgment. You don't find this promise in many Promise Card boxes, but if you deny him, he'll deny you—and if you proclaim him now, he will always say about you, "This one's mine."

47

An Arresting Kind of Belief

Remember the apostle Paul's testimony? He told the Romans, "I am not ashamed of the gospel, because it is the power of God for the salvation of everyone who believes" (Romans 1:16). Now that's just the kind of committed, sold-out believer God looks for—one with no reason to be ashamed of Jesus Christ and his sacrifice!

As a Pharisee, Paul had worked so hard, thinking he could earn God's favor, that it flat-out amazed him to learn that the Lord's grace was free. God sent an invitation to everyone in the world to the biggest social event of the universe! Paul couldn't keep this news to himself. It captivated him. In fact he called himself a "captive of Christ" long after Jesus said, "I call you friends."

So why is it that some Christians say they have God's invitation, then act ashamed of it, too embarrassed to tell their friends? What does that say about their belief? It doesn't sound like the same kind of believing Paul practiced, does it? What about you and me? What are we doing with the invitation?

Jesus always taught that sharing our faith with others is a mark of the Christian life. His last word to us before he left the earth was a command to go into all the world and share the gospel with everyone. Just a few days before he mounted the cross on which he would die, he told his disciples something I just can't get away from:

> Then the King will say to those on his right, "Come, you who are blessed by my Father; take your inheritance, the kingdom prepared for you since the creation of the world. For I was hungry and you gave me something to eat. I was thirsty and you gave me something to drink. I was a stranger and you invited me in. I needed clothes and you clothed me. I was sick and you looked after me. I was in prison and you came to visit me." Then the righteous will answer him, "Lord, when did we see you hungry and feed you, or thirsty and give you something to drink? When did we see you a stranger and invite you in, or needing clothes and clothe you? When did we see you sick or in prison and go to visit you?" The King will reply, "I tell you the truth, whatever you did for one of the least of these brothers of mine, you did for me."
>
> —MATTHEW 25:34-40

O Father, let your Spirit burn these words into our hearts! Let us be so flat-out amazed by your Son that we take off the old life of self-centeredness and put on the new life of loving and serving others like Jesus. Let us feed the hungry and clothe the naked, visit the prisoners and welcome strangers.

We're not saved by doing these good works, but Jesus said if we are saved our lives will produce good works. We'll have a new heart within, a new way of looking at people, and our new hearts will compel us to reach out to others. Like Paul, we'll be waiting to bless as we've been blessed, absolutely captivated by the love of Jesus.

48

HIS ASSURANCE IS SWEET

There have been times when I've doubted whether I was saved. I've thought: *Maybe I am not really a Christian. Maybe I'm only fooling myself. What if I get to the judgment and God says, "Sorry, I never knew you"*—because he will judge in righteousness, according to what we've done?

I've read about the surprised people who will be at the final judgment. The Father will look at them and ask, "Who are you?"

They'll say: "C'mon, Lord, you know us. We did lots of incredible things in your name. We said to demons, 'We cast you out in the name of Jesus,' and they left. In your name we prophesied, proclaiming the Word—and now you're saying you don't recognize us? There must be some mistake!"

The Father will say, "Sorry, I never knew you. It's too late. Leave my presence forever."

Knowing this, are my fears so unfounded? Paul mulled over this matter, too:

> Or do you show contempt for the riches of his kindness, tolerance and patience, not realizing that God's kindness leads you toward repentance? But because of your stubbornness and your unrepentant heart, you are storing up wrath against

yourself for the day of God's wrath, when his righteous judgment will be revealed. God "will give to each person according to what he has done."

—ROMANS 2:4-6

How can I know if I'm storing up wrath for myself? The answer is found in 1 John 3:18-19, which says that when Christians serve Jesus by serving others we have confidence that we're going to heaven. When we serve out of compassion and obedience, when we speak the gospel and live it, we have within us the guarantee that we are saved!

As John puts it: "Dear children, let us not love with words or tongue but with actions and in truth. This then is how we know that we belong to the truth, and how we set our hearts at rest in his presence" (1 John 3:17-19).

Think of it this way: God did not create people for the purpose of destroying them. No one plants a tree just for firewood—for shade, maybe, or fruit, but not just for firewood. Only when the tree becomes unfruitful or dies is it cut down and burned. Your life is the same. God planted you for abundant life. He looks for fruit—and he rewards it! After you've chosen Christ, the good work you do out of a pure love for Jesus assures you that God's at work in you.

When I doubt my salvation, I look at all the ways I am different now from the way I used to be. I know God is in my life because I can't make myself kind, generous, or patient. I know that when those things like kindness and patience are present in my life, it's because I have Jesus, the fruit-producer, living inside me. That gives me confidence and assurance to go on.

49

THE HEART OF THE
WEDDING FEAST MATTER

A lot of people get confused and start pushing other Christians around, telling them they're not saved because they missed a chance to witness to somebody or an opportunity to serve. They point to Jesus' parable of the wedding feast (Matthew 22) and preach that you can lose your salvation if you're not out there preparing for the feast to celebrate Christ, the bridegroom of the world.

This is a tricky area theologically because it's clear that salvation can't be earned. At the same time, it's also clear from Jesus, Paul, and the disciples that we are to produce good work in ourselves and toward others. So while it's never our business to judge who's in for God's great feast or who's out, it is our job to remind each other to change our clothes before the wedding.

That means I have to ask you, and you have to keep asking me: "How's your heart? Have you gotten hard or lazy? Are you making the mistake of saying, 'I accepted Jesus some time ago, and I used to lead a Bible study and introduced some people to the Lord back then—that's proof enough of my righteousness, isn't it?'"

No, Jesus wants us to live close to him so that we become more like him every hour, every day. He wants to be sure that when we stand before God to get into the wedding feast we're not just waving our invitations, but we're covered in Christ's robe of righteousness.

See, God's nature, his mercy, is like that robe offered to cover each one of us. God offers you his nature and asks you to take it on as your nature. So first you become righteous because he is righteous. Then his righteousness is worked into your heart. The process originated with God, but you have to take what he gives—righteousness and grace—and let it grow into your life. So the more righteousness, the more grace.

For example, when he shows you mercy, he looks to see if you are showing mercy to others. If you don't show mercy, it demonstrates that you don't honor or respect the robe of mercy that God's offered. So mercy is taken away from you because you threw it into the mud!

Jesus explained it this way: "Whoever has will be given more, and he will have an abundance. Whoever does not have, even what he has will be taken from him" (Matthew 13:12).

Man, it's so easy to forget that I'm supposed to be changing all along the way. That's why all I'm saying is it's not so terrible to keep God's righteous judge side in mind; it's not such a bad thing to strive to serve God better, more from the heart.

50

YOUR SPIRITUAL RSVP

If you were invited to a friend's wedding and knew it was going to be a dress-up deal, all formal gowns and tuxes, you wouldn't show up sweaty and dirty in your ditch-digging clothes, would you? To do that would be like saying to your friend, "Sorry, I knew your wedding was today, but my own work was more important than getting ready to honor you."

This is the point in Jesus' parable of the wedding feast (Matthew 22), where the king extends an open invitation for everyone to attend his son's wedding, and then he is harsh to the guest who comes in old clothes.

Think about it: Everyone was invited to the wedding feast in the clothes they were wearing, but they weren't supposed to show up that way to the formal feast. Accepting an invitation means you understand the place of welcome and honor that's offered to you, and you show your gratitude by dressing appropriately for the occasion. In the time between when the invitation was given and when the guests sat down with the king's son to celebrate, they were supposed to get ready to meet the king and his son.

God has invited us to feast with him and his son. The invitations with our names on it were written in blood—while we still were wearing our sin, rebellion,

and unfaithfulness. Do you see what an honor it is to
be invited into God's presence? Are you changed in
your heart because of it? Do you let yourself become
robed in righteousness because you're so humbled,
so thankful to be invited at all?

Standing before God is not a come-as-you-are
affair. Only one set of clothes is acceptable—the
robes of righteousness. God provides the clothes
you need for the feast. That's grace. You have no
righteousness outside of Jesus Christ, no way to
stand before God and be accepted on your own
merit. You must throw yourself on his grace and ask
him to change you and clothe you in his righteousness—and he will! Isaiah tells us:

> I delight greatly in the LORD, my soul
> rejoices in my God. For he has clothed me
> with garments of salvation and arrayed
> me in a robe of righteousness, as a bride-
> groom adorns his head like a priest and
> as a bride adorns herself with her jewels.
> —ISAIAH 61:10

Jesus ended the parable of the wedding feast with
the words, "For many are invited, but few are
chosen" (Matthew 22:14). The invitation to the marriage feast of the Lamb has gone out to everyone who
has ever lived. We're all invited because of the grace of
God, but we're chosen to be part of that feast by what
we do with that grace. It's a paradox that makes
sense when you realize God wants changed lives.
Paul knew this when he wrote: "...continue to work
out your salvation with fear and trembling, for it is
God who works in you to will and to act according to
his good purpose" (Philippians 2:12-13).

When we really enter into the righteousness of Jesus, we are changed. Then, when we get to the wedding, it will be easy for God and everyone else to see that we took the invitation seriously. We honored and respected God enough to come dressed in wedding clothes and ready for the party. John, the beloved disciple, saw this in the revelation God gave him of heaven:

> "Let us rejoice and be glad and give him glory! For the wedding of the Lamb has come, and his bride has made herself ready. Fine linen, bright and clean, was given her to wear." [Fine linen stands for the righteous acts of the saints.] Then the angel said to me, "Write: 'Blessed are those who are invited to the wedding supper of the Lamb!'"
>
> —REVELATION 19:7-9

51

Take This and Call God
in the Morning

A friend once said to me, "Even if there were no heaven or hell, I'd follow Jesus because being a Christian is the most exciting and fun life you can lead. God gives me everything I need. Hallelujah!"

Why is it some Christians see God as a big Sugar Daddy in the sky? They think God works 24 hours a day to make life smooth for us, to shelter us from anything painful or stressful, and to give us everything we want. They promise people that all their material needs and 95 percent of their wants will be taken care of when living for Christ.

Yet if the gospel promised a joyride through life, wouldn't everyone want to be a Christian? How does this attitude compare with the life of servanthood and suffering that Jesus led? How does it compare with the lives of Jesus' true disciples? Did Jesus see his life as fun and easy?

No, Jesus didn't look forward to his suffering. Matthew tells us:

> Going a little farther, he fell with his face to the ground and prayed, "My Father, if it is possible, may this cup be taken from me. Yet not as I will, but as you will."
> —MATTHEW 26:39

Jesus was scourged and beaten by the Roman soldiers. He hung in agony on the cross. It makes us sad, but we're grateful because Jesus' pain brings about our salvation. His suffering frees us from the load of sin and guilt we carry. His painful death gives us a new start.

That's where too many of us get confused. We think a new start means life on easy street. But Paul told the Philippians, "For it has been granted to you on behalf of Christ not only to believe on him, but also to suffer for him" (Philippians 1:29).

That's right. God has granted us to suffer like it's some kind of favor. Of course, this goes against what too many of us believe about God. In fact, upon hearing this some Christians immediately begin to rationalize: "There's no need for a Christian to suffer today. Jesus suffered on the cross to give us abundant life. He suffered once and for all so that none of us will have to feel sad, get sick, or be mocked."

Oh, we love the way the Gospels show us the power of Christ's life, but we don't want to follow him in the way he lived. Blessings, sure. But follow Christ in his obedience to God, even if God chooses to lead us through suffering? For all our talk about being God's end-time people, maybe instead we're just a generation of overindulged, take-the-easy-way Christians.

We can't take the gospel, the good news that God has created a way of salvation for us, and make it into a "gos-pill"! There's no wonder cure in God's plan to take away ry troubles are achieving us an eternal glory that far outweighs them all" (2 Corinthians 4:17).

52

WHAT YOU CAN
GAIN FROM PAIN

When trouble comes along what do you do? Do you rebuke it in the name of Jesus, then later wonder why God let you down because your troubles didn't instantly vanish?

The apostle Paul knew about troubles and suffering. He was not only beaten and jailed for preaching the gospel, but he sang in prison with a bloody back. He told the Corinthians: "For Christ's sake, I delight in weaknesses, in insults, in hardships, in persecutions, in difficulties. For when I am weak, then I am strong" (2 Corinthians 12:10).

What? Paul is content with all this terrible stuff happening to him?

Well, he doesn't say he's content because God had blessed him with a late-model chariot, or because of his home improvements, seminar curriculum, or career advancement. Paul says he was content with things we avoid like the plague: difficulties, persecutions, distress, insults.

How many of us would be content after going through what he did? How many of us would survive with our faith intact? What secret did Paul know about God's eternal purposes in suffering?

Paul's answer can be found in what he told the Thessalonians: "Be joyful always; pray continually, give thanks in all circumstances, for this is God's will for you in Christ Jesus" (1 Thessalonians 5:16-18).

Paul knew there was warfare going on, a spiritual resistance. Paul reminded Timothy that as a result of that resistance he suffered persecution while trying to help the young churches. Jesus faced the same resistance and died a criminal's death as an outcast. Anyone who desires to live godly in Christ Jesus will be persecuted (2 Timothy 3:12). We are not to be ashamed of the testimony of the Lord. Instead we are to join Jesus in suffering for the gospel (2 Timothy 1:8-9).

Because Paul understood God's purposes, he told the Colossians that he actually rejoiced in his suffering (Colossians 1:24).

Are you able to rejoice in your trials like Paul? When you begin to wonder if you'll make it through, think like Paul, who forced himself to face the challenge of suffering like a man charging though the gates of hell. He pushed himself, like a runner does, to endure the pain and always keeps his eye on the prize.

53

"Would" Works

God longs to build godly qualities in our lives. We need to realize that suffering is one of the major tools he uses to do this. Sometimes, though, we stop blaming the demons for our troubles and begin to murmur against God. We forget that our Lord was a carpenter who wants to chisel away our rough edges and create something beautiful. The minute things start getting tough, we complain, "God, this hurts too much!" We try to detour the Holy Spirit from his work.

Then God asks, "Do you trust me?"

We say, "Well, yes, of course, but you're not going to work on my selfishness or greed, are you? Why not teach me how to be a gracious and humble rich person instead?"

So we limp along with the same old sins year after year. We won't forgive somebody for what they did to us in the past, and we can't figure out why we're full of bitterness. So God sends more trials to reveal our bitter hearts. We cry and pray, "I rebuke this suffering in Jesus' name."

Again and again God brings us back to our hidden sin. He wants to reveal "the old man" to each of us. He wants each of us to say goodbye to the old man inside so we come alive in God. He wants each of us to say, "God, I don't care anymore. I want your life and your healing more than I want my own way. I'll lie still and endure this."

When we release ourselves to him, Paul reminds us, God's able to finish the job:

> We also rejoice in our sufferings, because we know that suffering produces perseverance; perseverance, character; and character, hope. And hope does not disappoint us, because God has poured out his love into our hearts by the Holy Spirit, whom he has given us.
>
> —ROMANS 5:3-5

So if you want to be a person of endurance, character, love, and hope, Paul says take hold of suffering and press through your trials with joy and faith.

Most of us would say, "Man, that's sick, isn't it?" But Paul considered it a privilege and an honor to suffer with Christ. He told the Romans:

> The Spirit himself testifies with our spirit that we are God's children. Now if we are children, then we are heirs—heirs of God and co-heirs with Christ, if indeed we share in his sufferings in order that we may also share in his glory.
>
> —ROMANS 8:16-17

See, your outward trials will begin to produce godly qualities within you—qualities like your heavenly Father's. Paul told the Philippians, "For it is God who works in you to will and to act according to his good purpose" (Philippians 2:13). God's good pleasure in us will not come through blessings or goodies, James says, but by sending trials and persecutions:

Consider it pure joy, my brothers, whenever you face trials of many kinds because you know that the testing of your faith develops perseverance. Perseverance must finish its work so that you may be mature and complete, not lacking anything.

—JAMES 1:2-3

Have you accepted Christ? Accept also that he will polish you into a person who radiates the fruit of the spirit. Take God at his Word and let his chisel of trials build these qualities in your life. God knows what suffering will build in you. Can you imagine what God could do in you if only you would let him?

54

AND NOW FOR THE LIFETIME ACHIEVEMENT AWARD...

Some people think that Christ's suffering means only his death on the cross. But Jesus suffered through his whole life on earth. He watched men and women live sinful, wicked lives, though he created us to be spotless and blameless. Then he had to deal with his disciples' constant lack of faith.

Imagine repeating the same simple message over and over, almost despairing that even his own friends and followers would ever understand: "O unbelieving and perverse generation...how long shall I stay with you?" (Matthew 17:17).

Jesus also had to deal with the rejection of his family because even his own brothers didn't believe in him (John 7:5). He wasn't recognized by his own people. John 1:11 says, "He came to that which was his own, but his own did not receive him." The Pharisees accused him and plotted to kill him (John 7:1; John 11:47-57). He was slandered and called an agent of Satan because he healed people (Matthew 12:22-29). Talk about being misunderstood!

As Jesus' disciples watched him go through all this, Jesus told them plainly that they could expect the same:

A student is not above his teacher, nor a servant above his master. It is enough

for the student to be like his teacher,
and the servant like his master. If the
head of the house has been called
Beelzebub how much more the members
of the household!

—MATTHEW 10:24-25

Let's face it. If we are called Christians, followers of
Christ, we have to follow him through the temptations and challenges in this world. We need to follow
his example in how we respond, too, which means
without sin, with no deceit in our mouths, without
retaliation or threats when others hurt us (1 Peter
2:21-23).

Like any mom and dad, Jesus cares for his creation, and grieves when we are troubled or when we
do things that cause us trouble—when we continually miss the mark. He's like a parent watching the
child he raised so lovingly get into drugs or something else destructive. We're like that rebellious
child who says, "It's none of my parents' business.
Why should they care? It's my life!" But parents
can't help but care, and because they care, they
suffer. That's why Jesus suffers when we turn our
backs on him and go our own way. Do we suffer with
Jesus this way, grieving over the lost humanity all
around us, grieving with our own failure?

If we live as Jesus lived, grieve as he grieved, and
are crucified (spiritually speaking) as he was crucified, we can also share in his glory. It's part of this
life, Peter said, and promises something for the next
life: "Rejoice that you participate in the sufferings of
Christ, so that you may be overjoyed when his glory
is revealed" (1 Peter 4:13).

55

YOUR FATHER WEARS
COMBAT BOOTS!

When U.S. Army recruiters look for soldiers to sign-on they don't say, "Come and suffer hardship. We'll grind you to a pulp so you can 'be all that you can be.'" They never tell you before officer training school that you're going to be harassed, overworked, and pushed to the extreme (and by your own people!) before they approve you to the rank of officer.

No, recruiters soft-sell it. They make it look glamorous and exciting because they know sweat, blood, and dirt don't sell.

That's the way most of our preaching is too: "Gosh! Don't tell people they're going to have to suffer to be what God wants them to be! Tell them the glory will carry them away."

I think, after all he went through, Paul would have been upset to hear these sales-oriented false promises. He told us straight: "Endure hardship with us like a good soldier of Christ Jesus" (2 Timothy 2:3).

Instead, we somehow mistakenly expect to live out our faith as though we're lying on a big overstuffed mattress. We want to lean back on a Posturepedic cross and take it easy. But the way I read my Bible, God is going to bring some real hell on earth and it will separate the sheep from the goats, the true Christians from the pew-warmers.

So God wants to make us battle ready, trained for the spiritual war—whatever form it takes in our lives. He knows there's a battle for every Christian in every generation. He knows how fierce it's going to be, and he knows how much we need to be trained to fight. He wants us to be ready, able to fight, not just dressed in the uniform proclaiming to be Christians with only our bumper stickers, T-shirts, and coffee mugs.

Think about it: Before soldiers go to war they are put through punishing training that's as much as they can stand. Because the government wants to be mean? No. Because their commanding officer wants new recruits to know how to avoid getting killed when they get to the battlefield? Yes.

That's like God—he'll use hard circumstances to train us for the times we live in. But when we receive his training, we will find ourselves out of trouble when the real battles come.

56

THERE'S A REASON
THEY'RE CALLED PUSH-UPS

Do you want to know Jesus better? Then, Paul said, learn to rely on Christ more and yourself less, especially in difficult times. Paul understood this from firsthand experience:

> To keep me from becoming conceited because of these surpassingly great revelations there was given me a thorn in my flesh, a messenger of Satan, to torment me. Three times I pleaded with the Lord to take it away from me. But he said to me, "My grace is sufficient for you, for my power is made perfect in weakness."
>
> —2 CORINTHIANS 12:7-9

You see? When Paul was at his most weak moment, when the most impossible odds were against him, then he could be the strongest because difficult circumstances forced him back to the Lord. "I can do everything through him who gives me strength," Paul said (Philippians 4:13), because it is Jesus who provides the power to get through troubles. In fact, that's how his power is made perfect.

In your weakness you're given the chance to stop trying to live on your own strength and admit you can't go it alone. Without a troubled time, then, there is little reason for most of us to lean into Jesus. It's so simple, but many of us miss the point and struggle on, sometimes for years, in our own strength. We're frustrated, ineffective, and powerless.

Finally we cry out to God, "O.K., you give me the strength!"

That's what he's wanted to hear all along because suffering conforms us to the image of Jesus. Trials and suffering push us until we come to the end of our strength. Paul explained it's at this point that we die to ourselves and allow Jesus to live through us:

> But we have this treasure in jars of clay to show that this all-surpassing power is from God and not from us. We are hard pressed on every side, but not crushed; perplexed, but not in despair; persecuted, but not abandoned; struck down, but not destroyed. We always carry around in our body the death of Jesus, so that the life of Jesus may also be revealed in our body.
>
> —2 CORINTHIANS 4:7-11

So you want more of Jesus and less of yourself? Then ask yourself this every day: Am I willing to go through whatever it takes to let that happen? Am I willing to be pushed to the end of myself?

57

I FEEL YOUR PAIN

Have you ever needed another's comfort? Good! Because suffering allows you to develop a deeper compassion for others. The problems and struggles you've experienced allow you to identify with those who also suffer.

One reason Jesus became a man was so that he could identify with us. Paul talked about this in his letter to the Corinthians, and we read about it in Hebrews too:

> Praise be to the God and Father of our Lord Jesus Christ, the Father of compassion and the God of all comfort, who comforts us in all our troubles, so that we can comfort those in any trouble with the comfort we ourselves have received from God. For just as the sufferings of Christ flow over into our lives, so also through Christ our comfort overflows.
>
> —2 CORINTHIANS 1:3-5

> For this reason he had to be made like his brothers in every way, in order that he might become a merciful and faithful high priest in service to God, and that he might make atonement for the sins of the people. Because he himself suffered

when he was tempted, he is able to help
those who are being tempted.

—HEBREWS 2:17-18

This is the abundant life that we're entitled to in
Christ—the suffering of Christ in abundance! Can I
hear a "hallelujah" on that?

The good news is that through our abundance of
suffering we can know the abundance of the Father's
comfort. When we receive his comfort, we have God's
comfort to give to others who are suffering.

58

Gardening Tips for Life's Thorns

Humankind may have started in a garden, but God never promised us a bed of roses—not on earth. That's why Paul pointed out that our struggles don't have much purpose without Christ's resurrection and the future with him in a glorious eternity. Looking back on his life, Paul wrote, "If for only in this life we have hope in Christ, we are to be pitied more than all men."

Did you ever consider that may be why God allows us to suffer? Do you see how knowing this helps us take our eyes off this world, which is not our final home anyway, and fix our hearts on the eternal joy set before us? Listen to what the Hebrews were told:

> Therefore, since we are surrounded by such a great cloud of witnesses, let us throw off everything that hinders and the sin that so easily entangles, and let us run with perseverance the race marked out for us. Let us fix our eyes on Jesus, the author and perfecter of our faith, who for the joy set before him endured the cross, scorning its shame and sat down at the right hand of the throne of God.

—Hebrews 12:1-2

In one way, then, earth is a training ground for Christians. The experiences we go through are meant to prepare us for our heavenly reward. This theme is repeated over and over in the New Testament. Jesus said to consider yourself blessed when you suffer for him because you will receive the same reward as the prophets, who also were cursed and are in heaven (Matthew 5:11-12). James said the person who perseveres will receive the crown of life (James 1:12). Paul encouraged:

> Therefore we do not lose heart. Though outwardly we were wasting away, yet inwardly we are being renewed day by day. For our light and momentary troubles are achieving for us an eternal glory that far outweighs them all. So we fix our eyes not on what is seen, but on what is unseen. For what is seen is temporary, but what is unseen is eternal.
>
> —2 CORINTHIANS 4:16-18

These Scriptures challenge us to look beyond earthly benefits now. Here, there is no promise of riches, pain-free living, or some big garden party. There will be temptations we must struggle to overcome and suffering to endure. But for those who resist lusts of the flesh and keep the faith despite trouble, there is an everlasting home, a final victory. At the final judgment, God will reward those who allowed him to build his character into them through hardship. The prize is that lasting thing—eternity with Christ, the Rose of Sharon.

59

THE SECRET WORTH TELLING

Do you know how Paul encouraged his converts? How he cheered them up? He reminded them
that we enter the kingdom of heaven through tribula-
tion, trials, hardships, disappointments, heartaches,
and rejection (Acts 14:21-22)—and he kept on
repeating that message in new places, to new listeners.

Can you imagine if I said to you, "Since I want to
encourage you and strengthen you, I'm telling you
that I see many trials ahead for you"?

I don't think you'd be encouraged at all! You'd
probably think, *God has forsaken me. Where are my
blessings? I'm cursed.*

Nobody wants to hear anything upsetting or
uncomfortable, anything that shakes a self-centered,
self-sufficient life. No, we tend to look upon trials as
an infringement. There are even those who say that
God wants us to enjoy outward peace and prosperity.

But how does this fit with what the Bible tells
us—that we will have inner peace and outer tur-
moil? Read Hebrews 12:5-10:

> "My son, do not make light of the
> Lord's discipline, and do not lose heart
> when he rebukes you, because the Lord
> disciplines those he loves, and he pun-
> ishes everyone he accepts as a son."

Endure hardship as discipline; God is treating you as sons. For what son is not disciplined by his father? If you are not disciplined (and everyone undergoes discipline), then you are illegitimate children and not true sons. Moreover, we have all had human fathers who disciplined us and we respected them for it. How much more should we submit to the Father of our spirits and live! Our fathers disciplined us for a little while as they thought best; but God disciplines us for our good, that we may share in his holiness.

Scripture tells us suffering is a blessing! We're children and heirs of God when we suffer with him. We don't need to make ourselves suffer, but when we're obedient to the Word of the Lord, we will endure adversity. Because God loves us, he takes the time to correct us. His discipline and chastening prepares us to enter into the kingdom of God. That was what Paul knew about suffering: It's a sort of training for the Lord. So when we greet adversity with the Lord's strength, we reap eternal benefits—peace, joy, inner freedom.

That was Paul's secret to holiness, and it needs to become our secret too.

60

Making Sense Of Discipleship

Jesus used some vivid images to show his disciples what we should be like—the light of the world, a city set on a hill, the salt of the earth:

> You are the salt of the earth. But if the salt loses its saltiness, how can it be made salty again? It is no longer good for anything, except to be thrown out and trampled by men. You are the light of the world. A city on a hill cannot be hidden. Neither do people light a lamp and put it under a bowl. Instead they put it on its stand, and it gives light to everyone in the house. In the same way, let your light shine before men, that they may see your good deeds and praise your Father in heaven.
>
> —MATTHEW 5:13-16

When you examine these things, you can understand more of what Jesus was getting at: A light is something others see. A city set on a hill gives others direction. Salt is something others taste.

Get it? Jesus wants his followers to be the visible, fragrant, touchable, flavorful expression of God to others. He wants us to be human expressions of him for others' sake. He knew many people wouldn't sit down and read the Bible, even if they were given one; the only Jesus they would see is the Jesus that lives in us.

Do people look at you—the way you live—and see Jesus? In every way are you growing, a living reflection of God so that others are drawn to him—not to you, but to the Lord?

That's what Jesus had in mind for disciples then, and he expects no less from his disciples today. It makes how we live each day more important than we realize. No matter what we do, our actions either draw people closer to Jesus or push them farther away from him.

Do we dare to continue living in a way that gives a distorted reflection of him? If we're serious about loving God and doing his will, then we have to do whatever is necessary to get our lives in order, and that means aligning ourselves to the Word of God. That is the only sure way we can present a clear picture of him! And when we imitate the character of God, others are attracted to what they see: faithfulness, integrity, and impartial love for every person. This is the flavor, direction, and refuge for life.

61

MADE WITH
REAL INGREDIENTS

Paul told the Ephesians to be imitators of God, not only smelling like him as a fragrant offering, as Ephesians 5:1 says, but letting our lives read like God's Word. Read what Paul told the Corinthians:

> You yourselves are our letter, written on our hearts, known and read by everybody. You show that you are a letter from Christ, the result of our ministry, written not with ink but with the Spirit of the living God, not on tablets of stone but on tablets of human hearts
>
> —2 CORINTHIANS 3:2-3

When I think of being an open letter to the world, I think of Richard Gene Lowe, a radiant example of God's goodness. When Melody and I met Richard, who was 84 years old, he had served the Lord for 70 years.

He lived in a little, one-room apartment filled with piles of clutter. He was never there to clean because he was always out helping others! He volunteered for many years at some evangelistic healing services in town, helping the people who came in wheelchairs. He saw many people walk out without those chairs, and he had amazing stories of

God's supernatural healings—his own and the healings of others. He really built our faith.

In fact, Richard was one of the first Christians we met, and the love and zeal he had for Jesus helped convince us that God was real and worth serving. Richard spent hours with us and our friends telling us about Jesus: how to talk to him, worship him, love him. Melody and I would run our errands or go to garage sales, and Richard would go with us or hang out in our van, always talking about Jesus.

Richard had hardly any money. He wore a $5, secondhand suit and he bought clothing at thrift stores, but not for himself. He gave those clothes to people in more need. Even though Richard didn't have a lot of material things, he freely gave whatever he did have, especially his time and love—and he gave it for the glory of the Lord and the blessing of others.

Richard is with the Lord now. But I have a feeling he'll be one of the first people to greet me and show me around when I get to heaven because he imitated Jesus and his faith was real.

62

HE WON'T PLAY ON OUR LEVEL

Paul said, "If we are faithless, [God] will remain faithful, for he cannot disown himself" (2 Timothy 2:13). But what does that mean?

For starters, it means even if we are faithless, God remains faithful because faithfulness isn't a quality he puts on and takes off on a whim. It's like his love and his holiness. He *is* love. He *is* holy. He *is* faithful.

God tells us, "You can walk away from me, ignore me, or misrepresent me, but I'm not going to break my promise to you because you broke your promise to me. I'll keep loving you and giving you chances right down to the finish line. If in the end you don't choose to return to me, then we'll both live the consequences of your choice. But don't expect me to come down to your level. I cannot be unfaithful. It's not my nature. I don't have a bailout plan if you break faith with me. I will continue on regardless."

This is amazing! Do you see it? God is faithful and will not break faith with us. He is light, as John said, and there is no darkness in him (1 John 1:5).

When he says, "I'll be faithful," he isn't keeping some secret clause buried in fine print in the contract. It's all on the table in plain view.

How different we are from God. If someone hurts us, we look for a way to strike back, right? Revenge?

If our friends gossip about us, we gossip about them. If someone hurts us, we think we have a right to do the same.

Well, John warns us that if we say we're like God but keep a little unfaithfulness tucked away in the dark, we're only lying. We're trying to fool ourselves and God.

Of course that won't work with God because Jesus said, "God knows your hearts" (Luke 16:15). But what about others? We've misrepresented ourselves to the world. We're not being light to them. Do you see why God places such a high value on faithfulness to him? He wants to know if we'll really be his hands and feet to the people around us who don't know him.

When we're not faithful, then we should beg God to teach us faithfulness, beg him to burn it into our character—and because of who he is, God will answer our prayer.

63

PLUGGING THE FAITH-O-METER

Quick, take this faithfulness test: How consistent are you? Can people rely on you? Can your friends count on your help when there's hard work to be done? Are you available and willing to help when things are going well and when they're not? Does your faith go up and down with the balance in your bank account? How do you react to God when your kids are sick? Does your love for God change according to your circumstances?

What about your faithfulness to those in your church? Do you only go to church when you feel like it? Do you make pledges to support missionaries or ministries when things are going well, then back out when you see a new car you want?

Yes, there is usually some personal cost for keeping commitments. It may cost time or it may take your money, but it always costs something. That's the nature of faithfulness. It means consistency.

That's what God wants with us. He wants us to be consistent in our love for him regardless of our circumstance. Sometimes we're quick to make commitments with our mouths, but we don't follow through with our actions.

Thank God that he is not like that. God can be counted on—he's not our friend one day and enemy the next. He's loving, kind, gracious, and compassionate. He demonstrated these attributes in Genesis, and he continues to demonstrate them today. He's never changed with the times and never promised anything he didn't do, no matter how much it cost him. He willingly sent His son to the cross to fulfill the promise made back in Genesis that he would send a Savior.

Talk about long-term commitment! And he hasn't quit yet.

What about you? Whether it's time, money, care, or energy, are you willing to pay the price of commitment?

64

THE FAITH THAT'S SEEN

The world needs to see a huge sunburst of faithfulness from Christians: faithfulness in our marriages, our financial dealings, and in keeping our word. One of the biggest tests of my faithfulness to God came through a Christian music company.

I had fulfilled my two contracts with my record company, and it was time to renegotiate. Executives from another larger Christian label started pursuing me with an incredible offer. They would set up a fund with $100,000 in it for each record I agreed to do with them. The cost of that album would come out of that fund, and whatever was left over from the $100,000 per album budget, I got to keep. So if one album cost me $40,000, I could put the remaining $60,000 into my own pocket as a personal bonus. The executives promised up to five albums with me using this agreement.

That offer was tempting. I had so many visions and goals for Last Days Ministries that could have been accomplished with that amount of money. But something didn't feel right. So I wrestled with a decision. On one hand I saw that the money was great. On the other, I knew I was going to make the albums no matter which company I signed with and what deal was made.

So no matter how I looked at this deal, I couldn't find peace. Somehow I felt the devil was trying to buy me off—and my ministry wasn't for sale. I didn't want to be seduced by all that money. I wanted to be faithful to the Lord. So I turned and ran the other way.

For me, it was the right decision. Jesus' parable about gold talents given to several servants helped me make my choice:

> Well done, good and faithful servant!
> You have been faithful with a few things:
> I will put you in charge of many things.
> Come and share the master's happiness!
> —MATTHEW 25:23

Right now Jesus is watching us, his disciples, to see if we are fit for bigger responsibilities. But not only is he watching, others are watching us, too. The question is: How are you going to let your light shine as an accurate reflection of our Father's faithfulness? The world waits for the answer only you can give.

65

THE PUBLIC AND PRIVATE LIFE OF JESUS

Did you ever notice how Jesus' enemies paid him a backhanded compliment? The Pharisees sent some of their disciples to Jesus, for appearance's sake, to compliment him. Their ulterior motive, however, was to trap the Lord.

"We know you are a man of integrity," the Pharisees' disciples told Jesus, "and that you teach the way of God in accordance with the truth. You aren't swayed by men because you pay no attention to who they are" (Matthew 22:16).

You see, even the guys most against Jesus acknowledged that he was a man who walked in truth. That's because Jesus acted the same way to all people, in all circumstances. He didn't have a dark side to his personality that he needed to hide. Jesus not only lived a life open for all to see, but he wanted his disciples to see him in every stress, time of relaxation, and both in public and in private.

Now that's integrity.

How desperate people are to see that same integrity displayed in their lives! Probably this is because human nature is to only let others see us in certain situations, or to invite people to be with us when we're in public, but not in private. Still there is this cry for integrity. Read how King David longed for it:

> Let the LORD judge the peoples. Judge
> me, O LORD, according to my righteous-
> ness, according to my integrity, O Most
> High.
>
> —PSALM 7:10

Do you dare ask God to do the same with you? Do you turn your witness on and off like a faucet? Is there integrity in your heart? Do you know that the word integrity comes from the same root word as "integrate"? So are you making the parts of your life work together in a complete and cohesive whole?

That's what God wants. He wants to break down the barriers you and I put up between work and home, Sunday morning and Monday night, between our public and private lives. He wants the way we treat our husband or wife and kids to be integrated with the way we pray at prayer meetings. He wants the way we divide up our income to be integrated with what we teach others about giving. He wants the way we speak to others to be as pleasing to him as the way we read the Bible out loud at church. He longs for an integrated people who allow truth to invade not just a few areas, but every area of their lives.

The temptation, of course, is to pick and choose which areas God works his nature into. You know, show off your strengths and hide your weaknesses. That's human nature because even before we became Christians we had areas of strength, special talents, and abilities; we also had flaws and characteristics we tended to ignore or tuck out of sight.

After we meet Jesus, however, the Holy Spirit begins to work. His aim is wholeness. He wants to bring us to a place where all areas of our lives are integrated and functioning for his glory. Imagine what God could do if we allowed him to use every part of you? Jesus opened all of his life for others to see. What would people see if you and I did the same?

66

You Can Plow Ahead
or Let God Smooth the Way

When I became a Christian, there were many weak areas in my life that I was happy to ignore. But Jesus wanted to bring everything into the open. He started to show me, and everybody around me, the weakest areas in my character. This was painful at first, but then I began to catch on. I saw what he was doing, and how it was for my own good.

Like a chain that is only as strong as its weakest link, my life was only as useful to God as my most unsurrendered and unholy area. So he wanted to make the weak areas of my life as strong as my strongest areas, and he wanted me to submit all of it to him.

I was not the first to confront this struggle. The Pharisees had tremendous strengths. Every day, their every action was dominated and scrutinized by Old Testament Law. Unfortunately the Pharisees' hard, legalistic hearts would sooner bind up others than free them. They allowed no room for God to work, so even their strength became their weakness.

Do you see? You can plow ahead in your strong areas and leave out the Lord who waits to fill in the valleys in your life. The result is self-righteousness.

Isaiah promised that when the Messiah came "every valley shall be raised up, every mountain and hill made low, the rough ground shall become level, the rugged places a plain" (Isaiah 40:4).

This, of course, didn't happen in a literal sense. The mountains didn't cave in when Jesus was born. But in a personal sense this change happens to people who follow Jesus in spirit. God wants to smooth out the rough edges in your life. He wants to take the tops off the mountains and use them to fill in the valleys until you're a balanced person of integrity. He wants your strengths to come under his authority, and he wants you to give him your weaknesses to let him fill in each one.

Think about it. With God's help you can be someone whose actions match his or her words, someone who's not hiding a weakness but exposing it to the light of God's truth. You can be a person of integrity.

67

LOVE HAS A FACE

Love. Oh, we do like to use that word. Sounds so sweet, right? But do we love so clearly and obviously like Jesus loved?

Jesus rescued the woman caught in adultery, and there never was any argument over whether she was guilty. By law, she deserved to be stoned! By law, there was no place to reconcile her or anyone to God. But Jesus challenged her persecutors about their own righteousness. He went beyond the law and loved.

Remember the Samaritan woman drawing water from a well? The disciples saw Jesus talking to her in an age when it was unusual enough to see a man speaking meaningfully to a female, let alone this Samaritan, a sworn enemy of the Jewish people! According to Jewish customs, Jesus shouldn't have anything to do with this woman. The disciples wouldn't have even touched the cup of water she offered because in their eyes it was unclean. But Jesus accepted what the woman offered and pointed her toward salvation.

The list goes on of who Jesus loved. The disciples saw him with every conceivable type of person, dealing with every conceivable reaction. But no behavior, no matter how bad, drove him away. Jesus was the same with everyone. He healed lepers and dined with Pharisees. There was no social group that he avoided; no one too educated or too ignorant for him to care about. No one rejected because of his or her age or religion.

Think about how out of step Jesus was with the society around him and how radical his actions were. People tried to trick him, challenge him on theological matters, and were ready to fight against him. But Jesus cut through all the labels people put on each other, spoke directly to the hearts of men and women, and he challenged his disciples to do the same.

How often do we look at superficial things and judge people without getting close enough to them to know what God's doing in their hearts? How often do we want to choose the social, age, or religious group that we prefer before sharing the gospel?

What an attitude. Our life is a reflection of Jesus to everyone we meet, not just those we select. We can't say, "Jesus, I'll witness to my friend Pete, but I'm not interested in Fred. He's a real jerk." The Bible says, "While we were yet sinners Christ died for us." When we choose to leave out some sinners because we think they're too difficult for the gospel, we're showing our ignorance of God's power—and we fail him as disciples. Jesus made it clear in the Sermon on the Mount:

> But I tell you: Love your enemies and pray for those who persecute you, that you may be sons of your Father in heaven. He causes his sun to rise on the evil and the good and sends rain on the righteous and the unrighteous. If you love those who love you, what reward will you get? Are not even the

tax collectors doing that? And if you greet only your brothers, what are you doing more than others? Do not even pagans do that? Be perfect, therefore, as your heavenly Father is perfect.

—MATTHEW 5:44-48

It's time for us to stop calling the shots about who we will go to and who we won't. Are we the hands, feet, and face of Jesus to the world or not?

When you turn on a light it shines all over the place. It doesn't say, "I'll shine three feet to the left and six inches to the right." Are you the light of the world or are you a hidden light? You decide.

As for me, I want God to polish me until others look into my face and see the face of Jesus reflected back. That's what it's going to take to call other people out of the darkness, not just words they hear like "Jesus loves you," but a face they see of acceptance and love.

68

Replaying Prayer

Some Christians think of prayer only as a way to get what they need from God. You know: They ask, he gives. Other folks think of prayer as a time to worship the Lord, or quote his promises, or stand in faith for what they need. Yet others think of prayer as a time to sit God down and remind him of their list of petitions. Too many of us even treat prayer like spray-on cleaner, as a way of commanding powers and principalities to be gone in the name of Jesus.

While prayer can be some of the above, do you think that's all that it is? What about considering prayer as the time when God reveals your heart to you?

Think about being alone and having one of those hidden surveillance cameras trained on you. What would your prayer time look like if you had to watch it played back on a screen? Would you be yawning and glancing at the clock to see how soon you could get out of there? Would you be arguing with God? Whining and complaining about his people? Letting God know how angry and disappointed you are that he didn't answer your requests the way you wanted? Would you only be praying when you're in trouble or need something?

If you take an honest, hard look at your prayer life, God will use it to sift through your heart. He will show you which of your attitudes align with those of the true servant of God, the one who really knows the master, and which attitudes don't.

Jesus urged his disciples to "get up and pray so that you will not fall into temptation" (Luke 22:46). He knew prayer would show you when your heart is pure and by that how to hear his voice, talk with him more wholeheartedly, and obey him more readily. What a combination! That's dynamite because then the Lord's prayer becomes yours: "[God's] kingdom come, [his] will be done on earth as it is in heaven" (Matthew 6:10).

69

WHAT TIGER'S
IN YOUR TANK?

Praying Hyde was a man convinced of the power of prayer. He would go to a town, rent a hotel room, lock himself in, pray for people, and whole towns would experience revival. Praying Hyde didn't even have to preach—just lock himself away and pray until people came under conviction of sin.

The secret Praying Hyde knew was that the all-powerful God always answers prayers. So when an answer seemed held up, Hyde didn't blame God or doubt prayer. Instead, he searched his own heart to find the problem. For instance, when he prayed for someone for two weeks and his or her life didn't change, Praying Hyde would bury his head in the pillow and cry: "O God, what have I done? Show me what sin has crept into my life that hinders you from answering."

You could say, then, that Praying Hyde was a man who took the words of Jesus literally when the Lord said: "Therefore I tell you, whatever you ask for in prayer, believe that you have received it, and it will be yours" (Mark 11:24).

Peter was that kind of man, too. He not only experienced the mighty power of God by offering prayer for others, but as the one lifted up in their prayers, too. Look at these two accounts:

> Peter sent them all out of the room; then he got down on his knees and prayed. Turning toward the dead woman, he said, "Tabitha, get up." She opened her eyes, and seeing Peter she sat up. He took her by the hand and helped her to her feet. Then he called the believers and the widows and presented her to them alive. This became known all over Joppa, and many people believed in the Lord.
>
> —ACTS 9:40-42

> So Peter was kept in prison, but the church was earnestly praying to God for him. The night before Herod was to bring him to trial, Peter was sleeping between two soldiers, bound with two chains, and sentries stood guard at the entrance. Suddenly an angel of the Lord appeared and a light shone in the cell. He struck Peter on the side and woke him up. "Quick, get up!" he said, and the chains fell off Peter's wrists.
>
> —ACTS 12:5-7

Do you really believe in that power—that prayer is effective? Or do you secretly think it's a waste of time?

Some Christians are like the Buddhists with their prayer wheels. They give their wheel a few whirls a day to make them feel pious. They pray so they won't feel guilty (after all, guilt takes all the fun out of life). They go through the motions, spin their wheels, and hope they've done their religious duty. But they never really expect anything to happen.

This is so far from the truth about prayer. Prayer is not a duty. It is a lifeline—the powerful gas in the tank that fuels the spiritual life. It's talking to God, listening to him, and then doing what he says. Prayer is close, intimate communion with the Lord, and it's the testimony of the church. Peter and Praying Hyde knew this, and they counted themselves God's friends and servants on earth.

What is your heart-attitude about prayer?

70

A Thought on Pure Prayers

You may think prayer is a powerless waste of time because you pray and nothing happens—and you may think that's God's fault. But think again. In fact, think about your motives for prayer. Are they selfish?

James said, "When you ask, you do not receive, because you ask with wrong motives, that you may spend what you get on your pleasures" (James 4:3).

That's very plain. You can pray for a lot of things that are right to ask for and that God might be happy to give, but prayer falls powerless when the person praying has selfish motives. That's right. Selfishness robs prayer of power.

For example, say a woman is praying for her husband to be converted. That's a good thing to ask of God, right? But how often is a request like this tainted with subtle, selfish motives? Does this woman want her husband to become a Christian so he'll stop drinking, swearing, and become more agreeable? Does she pray because her husband embarrasses her and she wants a spouse who makes her proud? Do you see the basis for those motives? In her heart, that woman has judged and despised her husband, and God wants to reveal such hatefulness and pride.

In the same way, praying for revival also pleases God, but it's possible to pray for even revival with a selfish motive. Let's say you want revival to increase your church's membership, or you want to make your ministry look good. Maybe you pray because you want to give a good report at your denomination's annual conference. Each of these reasons is polluted with a selfish motive.

So how do you pray with unselfish and pure motives?

Start by remembering the true purpose of prayer—that God will be glorified in the answer. That means when you pray for a spouse's salvation, pray because you can't bear the thought of your heavenly Father being dishonored, or because you can't stand to see the grace of God trampled underfoot. When you pray for revival, pray because you cannot stand for God to be rejected, or because you sense God's broken heart over the sin of unbelievers.

However you pray, God will know your motive. If you ask with a mind set on personal or corporate gain, even if it's a desire that's deeply buried, your prayers are hindered. Do you think God will give in to your selfish needs and wants? Think again. He loves you—and the whole world—too much to allow that.

71

THE ANSWER FOR
UNANSWERED PRAYER

When God wasn't answering the Israelites' prayers anymore, they came up with some interesting theories as to why not. They decided God was getting a little old. Maybe his hands had shriveled or he had arthritis, and didn't have the strength to reach out anymore. Possibly he was going deaf. What other reason should there be for their unanswered prayers? How could anyone trust a tired old grandfather in the sky?

Isaiah shook his head. You've thought of everything, he said, except the obvious:

> Surely the arm of the LORD is not too short to save, nor his ear too dull to hear. But your iniquities have separated you from your God; your sins have hidden his face from you, so that he will not hear.
>
> —ISAIAH 59:1-2

You see, Isaiah told the Israelites that God hasn't changed. He told them, "You have. Your sins are cutting off your communication with him. God can't hear what you're saying because of your sin."

Many of us have the same problem, and it crushes the life out of our prayers. We cry out to God in vain because there is sin that we know about but won't confess or forsake. Sometimes it's unconfessed sin from the past. Other times it's sin we're secretly indulging in now.

Either way, we forget the words of David: "If I had cherished sin in my heart, the LORD would not have listened" (Psalm 66:18).

But that's the beauty of prayer: If we ask the Holy Spirit to examine our hearts and, in turn, we confess our wrongs, God's always listening.

72

CLEAN FOR THE
CONVERSATION

I remember praying one time for two definite things. Both of these things needed to happen or God would be dishonored. I prayed and prayed, but the answer never came. The night before I needed God's answer I woke up in the dark. I cried out to God and reasoned with him about how I needed him to act.

Still no answer.

Again, I pleaded and begged. Finally, out of desperation, I asked God to show me if there was anything wrong in my life. Immediately God brought something to mind—sins he'd brought to my attention before, but I'd been unwilling to confess these sins I had justified.

"If that's what's wrong, then I'll give it up," I told God.

Now that's a pretty good prayer, but still no answer came.

"God," I cried again, "if that's sin, then I repent."

Still no answer. Finally I came out with it: "God, I acknowledge that as sin. I repent of it. I give it up." Within minutes, feeling at peace, I was sleeping like a baby.

In the morning the answer to my prayer came, and God's name was honored.

That experience taught me to pray like King David, a man after God's own heart: "Search me, O God, and know my heart; test me and know my anxious thoughts. See if there is any offensive way in me, and lead me in the way everlasting" (Psalm 139:23-24).

When I justified my sin I was stuck with it. But once I confessed and repented of it, I experienced a new power in prayer. I no longer needed to look for creative excuses for why God didn't answer.

If you want to pray powerfully, effectively, then you have to be ruthless about your sins, too. You have to let God put his finger on the things in your life that displease him. Believe it—God will reveal your sins. But know, too, that he delights to answer the prayers of those whose hearts are clean before him.

73

No Foolin'

There are times when I've felt like I was praying to brass walls. Even recently I got down on my knees, feeling flat and empty. I didn't try to work up any emotion. I didn't say, "Oh, Jesus, I'm going to worship you. I'm going to praise you." I didn't try to fool God. I just knelt there and said, "God, I can't pray. I don't even feel like praying. I come to you, not on my own merit, but in the name of Jesus."

And God whispered into my heart, "Okay, be quiet."

So I was quiet.

Then—bam! My emotions began to well, and I had a wonderful, peaceful time of fellowship with the Lord.

Such a powerful time would never have been possible if I'd tried to fake it with God—he already knew what I was feeling anyway. David wrote:

> O, LORD, you have searched me, and you know me. You know when I sit and when I rise; you perceive my thoughts from afar. You discern my going out and my lying down; you are familiar with my ways. Before a word is on my tongue you know it completely, O LORD.
>
> —PSALM 139:1-4

His psalms are probably the most honest prayers ever recorded; they're full of gritty reality. David takes us through the full range of human emotions. He is real with God. As a result, he experienced God's power in his life.

You can, too. You can pretend you're full of joy and love when you're not—but God already knows. You can't fool him into thinking everything is rosy, when you're really depressed and hurting or full of vengeful thoughts. Prayer isn't some kind of show. When you admit your frailty to God and rely upon him, he releases his strength and power to you, and that power will show itself in your prayer times.

74

IT'S ALL ABOUT HEARING

God doesn't care how eloquent your prayer is, how earnest you are when you pray, or even where you pray. What he cares about is whether you did the last thing he told you to do. See, doing all that God has told you to do is vital to having your prayers answered. It's called obedience, and without it, your prayers fall to the ground.

The prophet said: "Does the LORD delight in burnt offerings and sacrifices as much as in obeying the voice of the LORD? To obey is better than sacrifice, and to heed is better to than the fat of rams" (1 Samuel 15:22).

Often, though, we're unprepared for the mundane things God asks us to do. We want to hear him tell us to do spectacular, glamorous things—things that bring us glory, not him. But if we've hamstrung our relationship with him through disobedience, then our prayers will not be answered. He hears the prayers of the disobedient and says: That's such a fervent prayer. If only you would obey my voice with the same fervency, then I could really answer that prayer.

Now I wrestled with this for the first few years of my music ministry. I was really uncertain about how to handle the money I made because my music is just a tool to share Jesus. I reasoned: *I'm not in it*

*for the money, but the money did pay our bills—and
we had lots of food and big electric expenses because
of all the new Christians we took in to live with us in
several houses. Besides*, I thought, *I'm a minister,
not an entertainer. How much do you charge the
church to come and minister anyway? Is it right to
even charge anything?* These questions kept me up
at night because I wanted to hear God—and the
Lord spoke clearly to me.

I sensed God telling me to give free concerts and
take love offerings. If I was in a setting, like a fes-
tival, where an offering couldn't be taken, then I
could receive an honorarium. The Lord spoke simi-
larly to Buck and Annie Herring, formerly with the
singing group Second Chapter of Acts.

Now my concerts and those of the Second
Chapter of Acts were some of the largest Christian
concerts in America at the time. While the people
who came to the concerts were blessed, some folks in
the Christian music industry got upset. One agent,
who booked other Christian artists, was even angry.

He said, "If the high-profile artists do concerts
for free, it makes everybody else look bad."

That wasn't what I was trying to do. I was just
trying to be obedient to what the Lord told me to do.
I couldn't go back and say, "Well, God, I didn't obey
your first order, but give me another one and I'll do
better."

No, God wants obedience. Think of it this way.
Maybe God's impressed you to do something as simple
as making restitution to a person you've wronged.
Sometimes you say to God, "Oh, sure, but give me a
couple of days to pray about it." Think how God must
look at your response.

It's like one of my kids coming up to me and
saying, "What do you want me to do today?" What a

great question! All parents dream of their children asking things like that.

So I say something like, "Go out and wash the car."

But if my kid looks me right in the eye and says, "Well, let me go ask my dad," I'm going to say, "Hey, wake up! Here I am. I just told you to go wash the car."

See how futile this becomes? What you're saying to God when you keep on praying about something he's told you already is, "This isn't really what I had in mind. I'll just put it on hold and see if you will tell me what I want to hear." You don't pray about something God plainly tells you to do. You do it, and you keep the conversation going.

75

FIRST THINGS FIRST

Do you know what's just as serious as sin, or worse, that could be blocking your prayers? Idolatry—putting something else in place of God. "Son of man, these men have set up idols in their hearts and put wicked stumbling blocks before their faces," God told his prophet (Ezekiel 14:3). "Should I let them inquire of me at all?"

God is saying, "Why should I even listen to these people? They have idols in their hearts."

Do you have an idol in your life? Having an idol is a major block in your relationship with God, and it will kill your prayers.

Now, you don't have to have a little god set up in your living room, or make sacrifices on a pagan altar in your bedroom, to have an idol in your life. An idol is anything that takes the place of God in your heart, anything that becomes the object of your devotion: a wrong relationship, career, possessions, a new house, a car, and even your husband or wife or kids. My sinning can become an idolatry when I'm only asking for items on my prayer list and not praying to God. Religious practices can be an idol, too.

Even Bible reading can become idolatry if I'm doing it simply to get theological information instead of getting to know God better. In fact, there are some people who don't know Jesus at all but are enrolled in seminaries all over the country. They are people who have made the Bible their God. They worship the knowledge of God, rather than God himself. But God alone has the right to the supreme places in our hearts.

If your prayers are not answered, ask yourself this: "Is God first in my life?"

If not, it's impossible for us to prevail in prayer. God will not be second best in our lives, and he's always waiting, ready, lovingly, to be first.

76

OF PRAYERS AND POCKETBOOKS

Did you realize that stinginess hinders prayer? Scriptures show that if you don't respond to cries for help from God's children, then God won't respond to your cries.

Sounds legalistic, huh?

It's not. It's just that how you handle money reveals your heart. If God has your money, he knows he's got your heart. So now he wants you to be liberal in offering forgiveness, and with lending and giving your material possessions, time, and skills too.

It's not surprising that the prayers of some churches are not answered. Why should God bless a congregation who is only concerned with the color of the new pew cushions, the loan to build a new building, or increasing the pastor's salary—especially when the people should be pouring out their time, talent, and money to meet the needs of the poor and the needy?

Listen to this statement about prevailing in prayer in 1 John: "...and receive from him anything we ask, because we obey his commands and do what pleases him" (1 John 3:22).

What pleases God? King Solomon said it plainly: "If a man shuts his ears to the cry of the poor, he too will cry out and not be answered" (Proverbs 21:13).

It's that simple. Listening to the poor when they cry for help and responding to them. God responds to those who give to the poor. He answers their prayers, and pours out his blessing. See, the stingy person becomes powerless in prayer, while the generous person can become mighty in prayer.

77

His Will Is Positively Simple

Have you ever thought about how our most negative heart attitudes have a positive flip side? How our prayers will be answered when we pray with a pure heart and according to God's will?

John says, "This is the confidence we have in approaching God; that if we ask anything according to his will, he hears us" (1 John 5:14).

Isn't that amazing? That the way to prevail in prayer simply is to work with God? Of course, you need to talk with him and listen to him in order to know his will. But once you know his will, you can pray according to his will, and he promises to hear and answer. It's that simple. That's your confidence.

Despite being that simple, many of us still seem to miss it. We're busy asking for things that are selfish or self-indulgent, things that either don't have the best interests of others at heart or will bring glory to us instead of God.

Some of these things may not be bad. They're just outside God's will. For instance, we may pray, "If only you'd help pay my bills, Lord, then I'd do your will." God says, "Do my will. Do you know what it is?"

See, God looks for people he can reveal the desires of his heart to—people who will do his will joyfully. God hears and answers the prayers of these people and takes care of them.

Are you one of these people, or do you delight in doing your own will? If you'll only take off the blinders of self-seeking long enough and give God one minute, he can show you his will—for your life, the world around you, all the Christians in need, and all the people going to hell. Now, you may think that's a negative—putting your own will aside. But imagine the positives God promised: His will for your life is the only thing that will bring you ultimate fulfillment and joy. He has such great things in store for you.

78

WHAT DO YOU CRAVE?

There is no magic formula for effective prayer, but God does seem to answer the prayers from hearts desperate for Him.

Remember the accounts of this in the Old Testament? In Exodus 15:22-27, the people of Israel, in a desperate situation in the wilderness, were so thirsty they couldn't go on. The only water they found to drink was contaminated. There was no 7-Eleven where they could buy a soda to quench their thirst. So Moses cried out to the Lord, and the Lord showed him a tree. Moses cut the tree down and threw it into the contaminated water. The water was purified, and all Israel was able to drink.

That's the kind of desperation God wants from us. He wants us to come to the point where we're so thirsty for him to answer that we can't go on without hearing his voice. When he sees that kind of desperation, that we're totally dependent upon him and he is our only hope, then he answers every time.

James wrote, "You do not have, because you do not ask God" (James 4:2). James was saying, "You don't have because you don't crave it from God."

When was the last time you desperately craved God's answer to your prayers?

Maybe too many of us are still back at that place where we're blaming God for not answering our prayers, or in our hearts we think he's indifferent.

This was the case revivalist Charles Finney encountered at one congregation's town where he had prayed for revival. When Finney visited the church and listened to the prayers of the people, he was horrified. Every elder stood and prayed like this, "Oh, God, we have prayed now for many years and you have not answered. Lord, why aren't you answering our prayers? Why can't you hear us? Why have you not answered?"

Finally, Finney was invited to speak. He got up with an explosion in his heart. "Do I take it that you're blaming God for not answering your prayers?" he began. Then he preached about repentance from selfishness and sin.

At first, the congregation stared at him with cold and angry looks. Then one of the elders burst into tears, fell on his knees, and called out, "Brother Finney, it's all true!" The rest of the congregation did the same, and revival broke out.

For the first time, these people stopped blaming God for not answering their prayers and saw that the problem all along was in their hard hearts. Suddenly they craved what God wanted, what he had been waiting to give them all along.

Prayers should be answered. If yours haven't been, check your heart. Is it soft with love for God? Do you want to see glory and honor brought to his name from the answer to your prayer? Are you willing to obey his will and do what he tells you to do?

If you're not receiving answers to your prayers, it's probably not that God is saying "wait." More likely, it's that God is trying to get your attention, trying to

point out an area in your life where your heart attitude is wrong.

Ask God to reveal your heart to you. Correct the
areas that need correction and be fervent in prayer,
expecting and desperate for God to answer. You don't
have to settle for a powerless Christian life. God
wants you to prevail with prayers that bring the rule
of his kingdom to this world. In fact, he craves it.

79

TELL,
BUT SHOW FIRST

Jesus' disciple James challenges all of us who call ourselves Christians with this: You say you have faith? Where is it? Show it to me.

It's a good point, although a disturbing one, because faith is not something we can pull out of a drawer and spread out on a little velvet mat for people to admire. "Oh, look at Sue's faith. Isn't it great? It's much better than Danny's faith."

No, we can't isolate faith like that. So how do we show our faith in Jesus Christ? Read James' challenge carefully:

> What good is it, my brothers, if a man claims to have faith but has no deeds? Can such faith save him? Suppose a brother or sister is without clothes and daily food. If one of you says to him, "Go, I wish you well; keep warm and well fed," but does nothing about his physical needs, what good is it? In the same way, faith by itself, if it is not accompanied by action, is dead. But someone will say, "You have faith; I have deeds." Show me your faith without deeds, and I will show you my faith by what I do.
>
> —JAMES 2:14-18

Doesn't that stop you in your tracks? James says we can't get by with some of the pat things we say: "Faith? Oh, sure! I believe in my heart, but I don't think other people need to know about my faith. It's a private matter between me and God." What that attitude really says is: "I'm selfish. I'm only in this for me. I know I'm going to heaven, and that's all I was really after."

In fact, that's not really faith at all because faith is a gift from God—and he wants it to be so worked out in our lives that everyone can see it and give him the glory. Our faith should motivate us to reach out to others and tell them the good news—to give them food, visit them in prison, and open our homes to them.

We can't say we'll do the faith part and let someone who has a ministry of giving do the rest. There is no class of super-Christians who have faith and others who just naturally have a servant's heart.

James said: No way! Faith isn't a printed-out recipe. It's the active ingredient! Without works your faith is dead, fit to be buried. Faith must produce a change in the way you live. You must show your faith by the things you do with the money, time, and talents God's already given you.

That doesn't mean to do things to prove to God that you're good enough for him to save. No, that's what James calls dead work. It's not enough to go around giving tracts to the hungry, dying, homeless, and helpless, or to smile at them and say, "Jesus loves you." You can't offer salvation to people but never stop long enough to look at them with compassion as Jesus did. You can't forget to feed them so that their stomachs will stop gnawing long enough for them to hear the gospel.

How can anyone see a spiritual need but overlook the physical ones? William Booth, the founder of the Salvation Army, wondered this. He said that no one who had a toothache could really pay attention to the Gospel.

That takes a deeper commitment, doesn't it?

We're not on this earth just to tell others the good news. We're here to be living examples of the good news for everyone to see. Paul tells us, "For we are God's workmanship, created in Christ Jesus to do good works which God prepared in advance for us to do" (Ephesians 2:10).

80

AN IDEA FOR THE ROAD

Once the Lord told me to give a guy a lift all the way from Hollywood, California, to Tucson, Arizona. We'd met through a mutual friend, and this guy was genuinely nice but he didn't know Jesus. So when I learned he needed to catch the bus to Tucson the next day, I heard the Lord say to me, "You take him."

Now, when I offered this free ride for several hundred miles, this guy thought I was crazy. So did my friends. But this man was ripe for Jesus. So I preached all the way to Tucson, and along the way this new friend gave his heart to the Lord!

It was an out-of-the-ordinary thing to do, but my obedience to the Lord and giving of my time helped God reach another soul for his kingdom. It also made me consider these questions more seriously and regularly: Am I really interested in the good works that Christ has planned for me to do? Am I open to a faith that is living, active, and changes me into a willing servant?

To be willing means to become God's bond servant, so that everything I am and all that I have is at God's disposal. That's not to say I run out and give all my possessions to the poor just to prove I'm a radical Christian. Trying to prove something to God is a dead work.

Besides, the purpose of being a bond servant isn't about proving. It's about gratitude. It's about seeing that all we own belongs to the Lord because it was his to begin with, and he's only made us stewards. God gives us our bodies, time, and possessions so that we can use them to bless and minister to other people. And that's what I'm talking and thinking about these days: When it comes to the rubber meeting the road of how I live out my faith, how can I show that faith to others in practical ways so they'll be blessed by it?

81

What Universe Do You Live In?

There was a rich man who was dressed in purple and fine linen and lived in luxury every day. At his gate was laid a beggar name Lazarus, covered with sores and longing to eat what fell from the rich man's table. Even the dogs came and licked his sores. The time came when the beggar died and the angels carried him to Abraham's side. The rich man also died and was buried. In hell, where he was in torment, he looked up and saw Abraham far away, with Lazarus by his side. So he called to him, "Father Abraham, have pity on me and send Lazarus to dip the tip of his finger in water and cool my tongue, because I am in agony in this fire." But Abraham replied, "Son, remember that in your lifetime you received your good things while Lazarus received bad things, but now he is comforted here and you are in agony."

—Luke 16:19 25

Sometimes I deceive myself into thinking I'm better than the rich man. I think: *If someone was left outside my door, of course I'd take care of his or her needs.* How is it, then, that people are starving a few thousand miles away from where I live and yet I think, like maybe you do, that it's okay to ignore them?

Does God care that people thousands of miles away are starving, while we go on living in abundance? Do we think that because a famine or disaster happens in some part of the world where we don't see it everyday that we're not responsible to help?

To God, there is no distance. The ends of the universe are his walls. Since we are his children, what happens within his four walls should concern us, too. The father has chosen us to be his hands and feet to minister to people anywhere we know there is need and hurt. As for giving from our riches, whatever they may be, if we don't think about that in this universe, it's sure to become a hot topic in the next.

82

To Whom It May Concern...

In the evenings, don't we love to sit in our air-conditioned living rooms and watch TV? But there, on the news, how often do we see the faces of dying, starving, helpless people—people afflicted by war, famine, disease, and other disasters?

These people aren't being laid at our gate or even on our doorsteps. They're brought right into our living rooms! They look us straight in the eyes while we kick back in our cushioned recliners and say: "Could you bring me some more gravy, dear? My goodness, look at these starving people! Would you mind changing the channel? This is upsetting my dinner!"

Sometimes they look at us from the mail we pick up each day. The first thing many of us do with our mail is to sort out the junk. But do you know what we're counting as junk mail? The pleas for help from relief agencies. The request for funds for an unwed mother's home. The missionary writing about a need for increased support.

These things are laid at our gates, and we throw them in the trash can.

You can say, "Well there's a limit to what I can give." But I sense God asking, "Okay, what's the limit? Who set it?"

What is the limit of your concern? Are you going to leave the homeless and starving lying helplessly on your living room rug?

God will require you to account for every need you turn away and when you're too selfish to care. Jesus made it pretty clear. He said the person who has two coats should give one to the person who has none (Luke 3:11).

Now, maybe you don't personally know someone who has no coat, but in today's media-oriented world, can you really say, "Hey, I didn't realize there were people out there in the cold or people out there suffering and starving"?

If we didn't know about these needs, we might have an excuse. As Jesus said to the Pharisees: "If you were blind, you would not be guilty of sin; but now that you claim you can see, your guilt remains" (John 9:41). Or, as his disciple James put it on an even simpler level: "Anyone, then, who knows the good he ought to do and doesn't do it, sins" (James 4:17).

83

Is Ministering in Your Nature?

It's not easy ministering to people's needs because it's not natural! Our flesh tries to think of ways to get out of it. We have endless justifications and excuses for not doing what God has told us to do. Listen to this from Luke 10:25-29:

> On one occasion an expert in the law stood up to test Jesus. "Teacher," he asked, "what must I do to inherit eternal life?"
>
> "What is written in the Law?" he replied. "How do you read it?"
>
> He answered: "'Love the Lord your God with all your heart and with all your soul and with all your strength and with all your mind,' and, 'Love your neighbor as yourself.'"
>
> "You have answered correctly," Jesus replied. "Do this and you will live."
>
> But he wanted to justify himself, so he asked Jesus, "And who is my neighbor?"

Jesus knew this guy's heart, and he knows ours, too. So he told the story of the good Samaritan. Most of us know it—how the priest and the Levite both hurried on the other side of the road to avoid the man who had been robbed. We know that it was a despised Samaritan who took pity on the man who had been assaulted. After Jesus told this story, he asked the lawyer who provoked it (Luke 10:36):

> "Which of these three do you think was a neighbor to the man who fell into the hands of the robbers?"
> The expert in the law, "The one who had mercy on him."
> Jesus told him, "Go and do likewise."

Go and help. It's a commandment that's repeated over and over in the Bible. How, then, can any of us say: "It's not my responsibility," "I don't have a burden for this person," "I don't feel led," or "It's not my ministry"? Can God really dwell in a heart that's so closed to the needs of other people? John's answer was pretty blunt:

> This is how we know what love is: Jesus Christ laid down his life for us. And we ought to lay down our lives for our brothers. If anyone has material possessions and sees his brother in need but has no pity on him, how can the love of God be in him?"
>
> —1 John 3:16-17

So Jesus commanded us to reach out to the poor and needy, and we know who those people are. The question now isn't, "How can I serve where it's easy or where, given my human nature, it feels natural?" No, the question we need to be answering with our lives is, "What am I doing for those in need?"

84

When Little Things Mean a Lot

Don't fool yourself. When you begin to obey God, you will need to make radical changes in your lifestyle. I learned this when God began to deal with Melody and me about eating out less. God convicted us that, if at all possible, we were to eat at home more.

Sure, it's nice to have somebody else cook, deliver a meal to your table, and clean up. But we became convinced that it was a waste of God's money to pay somebody to do for us what we could do easily for ourselves. So we began making our own meals for about a third of what it had cost to buy them in a restaurant. We gave the money we saved to help the poor. It was such a little thing, but it came out of our changed hearts.

Everyone can ask God to show them some way to do similar things. God is looking for people who will put themselves and their resources—and not just more leftovers—on the altar for his use.

In fact, Jesus rebuked the Pharisees for merely giving out of their excess. That would be easy giving. Jesus commented on this when he saw these very pious guys giving the equivalent of $1,000 to the temple treasury, and then a widow came along and put two cents in the collection. Such a little thing for her to contribute, right? But Jesus said,

> I tell you the truth, this poor widow
> has put more into the treasury than all
> the others. They all gave their wealth;
> but she, out of her poverty, put in every-
> thing—all she had to live on.
>
> —Mark 13:43-44

In light of the poor widow's generosity, the Pharisees' giving is like when you no longer need something like a coat, so you give it away. The person who receives the coat needs it and says, "Praise God!" So you think you've obeyed Scripture and given in generosity. But the truth is you gave away something you were ready to throw out. You gave it away to make room for the new leather coat you really wanted. That's not sacrifice or the kind of lifestyle Jesus wants you to live. The Lord wants you to use everything he's entrusted to you, and your generosity shows you believe what you say—that you've, in turn, entrusted your whole life into his hands, that your faith is not in vain.

It's easy to out-give a rich man. All you have to do is give from your heart, even if what you give seems a little thing. Jesus doesn't look at the amount you give. He looks at what it costs you.

85

SERVE AS ONLY YOU CAN

Many Christians are like the rich man in the story of Lazarus (Luke 16:19-25). They're too busy with their splendid living to help those in need. Sure, these believers do "Christian" things, but they never focus their hearts on people who need help; they have no idea that it's possible to hallelujah, praise-the-Lord, and bumper-sticker your way to hell.

I, too, have struggled, especially with knowing how many material things to own here on earth. I know I should be like Jesus, who constantly ministered to those in need and never left a record of things he possessed. Instead, we know what he gave away and who he helped. I know Jesus never said living like this would be easy or that I could figure this out on my own. I know I need God to guide me. But it's easy to get bogged down on just keeping the rules of Christian living.

People thrive on rules—rules for this, rules for that. We're so busy keeping the rules that sometimes we miss the Spirit's leading. Jesus never made up a set of rules for us to keep. He's interested in whether we hear his voice and obey it. If we listen to the leading of the Spirit, he'll show us how to relate to the material things we own.

Jesus said if we are his sheep we will hear his voice (John 10:27). He told the disciples that he would send a comforter—the Holy Spirit—who would lead them into all truth (John 14:16).

So while Jesus wants us to follow him with our whole hearts, he knows that means different things to different people at different times.

For example, Jesus told the rich young ruler to sell all his possessions and give the money to the poor (Matthew 19:21). The New Testament doesn't record Jesus telling anyone else to do that.

In Matthew 26:6-13, read about the woman with the jar of expensive perfume. She poured it over Jesus' head, and the disciples were disgusted. They said, "What a waste." They thought about all the other things they could have done with the money it cost to buy that perfume.

But Jesus rebuked them. He said, "The poor you will always have with you, but you will not always have me."

Was Jesus contradicting himself? Was he being inconsistent?

No, he meant that we should never love the poor more than him. "Love me in the poor," he was saying. "Whatever you did for one of the least of these brothers of mine, you did for me" (Matthew 25:40).

We've all been called to serve the poor. But only you can answer God as to how you will do that. When you see how you are to serve the poor you are answering to Jesus how you are going to serve him

86

ARE YOU LISTENING TO FRIENDS IN HIGH PLACES?

We love to sing the hymn, "I Have Decided to Follow Jesus," especially the part that goes: "Though none go with me, still I will follow." But we don't practice it. Someone gets a bumper sticker that proclaims their beliefs, and pretty soon we've all got bumper stickers. Someone tells us it's spiritually mature to pray a certain way, so we all do it that way. If other Christians started riding to church on Pogo sticks with little fish on them, we'd be doing it, too.

Unfortunately, other Christians often hold us back from doing the will of God. It's easy to be molded into each other's images, and difficult to be molded into the image of Christ. But who do we want to please more? Each other or God?

I thought about this recently because I realized that if I used the Bible as my only standard for living, I'd be living a lot differently. What keeps me back, though, is the way I serve the opinions of other Christians more than I serve God.

The opinion of a person who is far away from God doesn't worry me so much. I'm not so concerned if an unbeliever says, "I don't like the way you said, 'Praise the Lord.'" That wouldn't stop me from saying it. But if a Christian says, "Brother, I don't think that's the way the Lord would have us do it," I feel condemned. It's the response of other Christians and my own sinful need for their approval that can make me change the way I serve God.

The thing I've realized is that I need to get my eyes off others, even other Christians, and back on the Lord. I'm on this earth to please him, not other people.

What about you? Living the lifestyle of a disciple of Jesus requires that you ask yourself some basic questions: Am I willing to open up my home and wallet? Am I willing to allow needy people to come in and maybe dirty up my new carpet and sofa? Am I willing to be inconvenienced for the sake of others? Will I let people come in and invade my privacy? Am I willing to follow Jesus to the point of being ridiculed by others, even my Christian friends?

87

Invest Yourself

If you listen to a lot of preachers today, you'd think that God wanted nothing more than to fill our pockets and bank accounts. I've even heard a story preached about a Christian who died and went to heaven. God took him into a room and opened a huge cupboard full of emeralds, diamonds, and every other precious stone you can imagine.

"Wow!" the man said. "Are all these things for me?"

God shook his head. "No. That's all you could have had. It's the reward I wanted to give you when you got here."

Where do we get this idea of reaping riches when we do God's will? And what kind of reward is waiting for us in heaven? These are sobering questions, but the answers from some Christians are polluted with compromise and hypocrisy, and are far away from what the Bible teaches. Jesus told us to lay up treasures in heaven (Matthew 6:20). He never built up treasures on earth—and told us that we shouldn't either. About our resources, all our possessions, wealth, talent, time, and abilities, he did say this:

> But the one who does not know and
> does things deserving punishment will
> be beaten with few blows. From everyone

who has been given much, much will be
demanded, and from the one who has
been entrusted with much, more more
will be asked.
—LUKE 12:48

So the Lord does keep account of what and when
we give. Also he says, Put it on my bill. I will take
care of it. You will get back your investment.

So, no, it's not what we give that saves us, and yes,
we are saved by grace and not works. But our works
prove that we are saved. An apple tree becomes an
apple tree as a gift from God. But the tree proves it's an
apple tree by producing apples.

Wise Solomon put it this way: "He who is kind to
the poor lends to the LORD" (Proverbs 19:17). This is
the only place in the Bible where it says we can lend
to the Lord—not give, but lend, which implies we'll
be paid back.

You see? God wants to invest us. When we put
ourselves and all that we own at his disposal, he
makes the most of us. Jesus said it this way:

But when you give to the needy, do not
let your left hand know what your right
hand is doing so that your giving may be
in secret. Then your Father, who sees
what is done in secret, will reward you.
—MATTHEW 6:3-4

In some ways, money and possessions are the
ultimate test of our faith. Jesus said, "No one can
serve two masters....You cannot serve both God and
Money" (Matthew 6:24).

Are you mastered by money, time, or anything
else you possess? Does your money serve God, or
does it control you? You may think you're the

master of your wealth, but are you using it to buy peace or to please God? You can let yourself become preoccupied with splendid living, or let God be the master of your money and all that you own. Either way, God will hold you accountable.

Wouldn't you rather store up treasure for heaven? This kind of living will not only radically change your whole life here, but it promises an eternal reward there.

88

There's a Reason
It's Called Cold Cash

There's a story I love to tell about a woman who lived in a typical suburb. She had struggled for enough money to make ends meet. At two o'clock one afternoon, as she was looking over her checkbook balance, there was a knock at the door. She found a strange man on her doorstep. He smiled, took a $100 bill out of his wallet and gave it to her. "There must be some mistake," she said, "I don't know you. This can't be for me."

"This is number 552, isn't it?" the man asked.

"Well, yes, but—"

"Don't ask the questions," the man insisted. "Just accept the money. It's for you." Then he turned and walked away.

The woman stood in her doorway staring at the $100 bill. She was overcome with joy and gratitude. She called up all her friends and told them what had happened. She was so excited she couldn't sleep that night.

The next day, at the same time, there was another knock on her door. It was the same man, holding another $100 bill! "Why are you doing this?" she asked.

"It's just something I want to do for you," was all he said.

"Are you going to come back?" she asked. "Will I see you tomorrow?"

"Maybe," he replied.

This woman went out and bought the biggest thank you card she could find, and she baked cookies to have ready in case the man showed up again. Sure enough, the next afternoon at two o'clock, the man was back with another $100 bill. She gave him the card and the cookies, then started baking more cookies for the next day. It was her way of showing gratitude.

Four days, five days, six, on and on it went. Every afternoon at two o'clock the man was there with a $100 bill. This lady was thrilled. Every day she waited expectantly for the man to arrive. After several months, though, she got tired of baking cookies. Besides that, having to be home every after-noon was a hassle. Getting the money was a blessing, but it took so much of her time. So she typed a letter to the man: "I'm sorry that I'm not at home to receive the $100 bill. Please leave it in the envelope provided, and slip it under the door. Thank you. P.S. I can't bake anymore, either. You appear to have plenty of money, so if you need more cookies there's a wonderful bakery on the next block."

For a few days this seemed to work, but one day there was no money in the envelope. The woman pan-icked. She needed the extra income. Her credit cards were maxed, she had new shoes on layaway, and what about the vacation home she was saving for?

The following day she stayed home to see what had gone wrong. At two o'clock she peered through the window and there was the same man, knocking on her neighbor's door. "Wait!" she yelled as she ran out to him. "You have the wrong house!"

The man turned and gave her a puzzled look. "This is number 554, isn't it?" he said. "It's your neighbor's turn. Why do you look so upset?"

Do you know anyone like this woman? What about you? Have you taken a long look at your life recently and thought, "Gee, where did God go? He was here a few days ago...or was it last week?" Have you felt cold toward God lately?

Spiritual coldness is a problem we all have to watch out for because we're all a bit like this woman. It's easy for us to live the Christian life when we're brand-new babes in Christ and the blessings are coming in like $100 bills. God seems to constantly bless us, and we seem surprised by his faithfulness and generosity. We say, "Wow! We don't deserve this," or "This is incredible! What can we do in return for you, God?"

So God says that he wants us to tell others about him. We say, "Sure we'll go do that right now."

Then the Lord tells us he wants us to give our cars to brothers in need. We say, "No problem, anything else we can do for you?"

But as we go on, we get used to the blessings flowing in every day. Our attitudes change. We begin to think, "You gave us that as a blessing. Surely you don't mean for us to give it away. We thought it was all for us." Paul told the Galatians:

> But now that you know God—or rather, are known by God—how is it that you are turning back to those weak and miserable principles? Do you wish to be enslaved by them all over again?
>
> —GALATIANS 4:9

It's easy to take God for granted. We forget what it was like before we knew Jesus. Our enthusiasm begins to fade. We become dry and hard-hearted. But the solution is simple: We can focus on the gift or we can focus more on the giver.

89

In Search of Happiness

I've seen a lot of people give their hearts to the Lord, thinking it would be smooth sailing from there. One guy came to our home fellowship and prayed the sinner's prayer. He was totally gung-ho—for about three weeks. He went out preaching on the streets and witnessing. But when he hit some opposition, and all his friends didn't think he was so cool anymore, he decided this "Jesus stuff" wasn't for him.

He was a lot like the seven churches that Jesus judged in John's revelation. Of one church, in Ephesus, Jesus said:

> I know your deeds, your hard work and your perseverance. I know that you cannot tolerate wicked men, that you have tested those who claim to be apostles but are not, and have found them false. You have persevered and have endured hardships for my name, and have not grown weary.
> —REVELATION 2:2-3

Now this sounds like a description of the perfect church, doesn't it? How could things be any better? These people worked hard at the Christian life. They stayed away from evil. The church tested anyone who came into the fellowship to see if they were for real, and this church had a 100-percent success rate at spotting false apostles! The congregation even suffered all sorts of problems and was ready to face more. These were mature Christians, right? They were impressive, weren't they?

Well, God wasn't happy with them. Jesus told them, "Yet I hold this against you: You have forsaken your first love" (Revelation 2:4). He was saying: "The truth is that something here has died and turned rotten. You don't have the sweet innocence and love that you started with; you're serving me out of habit and duty. You expect me to do all these things for you, but there's no heart left in our relationship."

The sad truth is the world is filled with people who have made a stab at being Christian. When Jesus doesn't pay like they expect, they split, saying it didn't work for them. All they wanted was an easier life, anyway. But as Jesus told the Ephesians: All the wonderful things you do right mean nothing in comparison to losing your first love for God.

Ask yourself: Am I looking for God to make me happy? Or do I want to belong to God, to honor him, and think of how to make him happy?

90

Get Real

Do you find yourself going through all the motions of religion, using all the right clichés and Christian expressions? You know, the right tone of voice with the right smile on your face?

Well, you can smell like a rose on the outside but inside still be a garbage heap. I know this because I fall into this sin myself.

It's easy to do. When most of us came to the Lord, we knew we were totally helpless. After we received him into our lives we wanted to spend as much time with him as we could. We wanted to talk to him about everything and study the Bible. We loved to fellowship with other Christians, too.

But three or four years later, we've learned our Bible; we know how to pray, worship, and praise the Lord. We can speak fluent Christianese: We know how to "feel led" or "have a burden" and "put things on the altar." We know all the right words, so we feel pretty good about ourselves. We keep it together.

There's only one problem. Our old pride has taken over again, and our hearts have turned stone-cold. Suddenly we don't need Jesus anymore.

You don't think this can happen to you? Let's say as a new Christian you got irritated enough with someone to yell. You'd feel so terrible that you'd confess it to God immediately: "I blew it. I just ripped

Joe to shreds." You'd feel bad about the situation so you'd make it right. But slowly you get sophisticated. When you get mad at Joe, no one knows except you, and you're not yelling anymore. No, you just avoid Joe. You make snide comments to other people about what a rotten job he's doing. A little slur here, a little gossip there, but you're not mad at Joe. No way! That wouldn't be Christian! Sound familiar?

If you keep up such false fronts, the rot only continues. Before long, you give up on being a lover of God. You lose the intimacy with him. You say to yourself, "Who needs the Spirit? Let's finish in the flesh."

Well, you can fool yourself, and you can fool others, but you can't fool God.

91

THE GOOD NEWS IS
HE DOES IT HIS WAY

Have you ever had someone make a major decision for you without consulting you? I've had people say to me, "Well, Keith, I told so-and-so that you would do this because I know that's what you want to do."

I raise my eyebrows as they stammer: "Well, um, I've known you for two months and, uh, you always do it that way. I, uh, guess I just thought that's the way you'd do it again."

No one can make a commitment for you without asking you first, isn't that right?

So how do you think God feels when Christians do that to him? Every day you and I say, "God would want me to teach the Bible this way," or "From what I know of God, I'm positive he'd want me to take this job."

We may guess right some of the time, but God doesn't want us to second-guess him on his will for our lives. So where is God while these decisions are being made for him? Is he out of touch? Inaccessible? Deaf?

The sad thing is his spirit is right inside us. He can't get any closer to us than that. God has made having a relationship with him as convenient for us as possible, and yet we let our love of him go cold by straying from him.

No one deliberately sets out to go off the path. But the truth is that living the deeper Christian life with Jesus takes more time, effort, and breaking of our will to continue in the Spirit than often we're willing to give. It takes our all, so we come up with the good idea of rules. After all, isn't it easier with our nature to keep a list of rules? Paul warned the Galatians:

> You foolish Galatians! Who has bewitched you? Before your very eyes Jesus Christ was clearly portrayed as crucified. I would like to learn just one thing from you: Did you receive the Spirit by observing the law or by believing what you heard? Are you so foolish? After beginning with the Spirit, are you now trying to attain your goal by human effort?
> —GALATIANS 3:1-3

You see, Paul was writing to a group of converted Jews. That's why he asked them if they received the Spirit by works of the law or by faith. As their faith and their first love for the Lord petered out, these converts fell back into what was familiar to them—legalism. They started to worry again about circumcision and keeping all the other commandments and rules.

Now, you and I don't do exactly the same thing. When our walk with the Lord gets dry and dead, we don't think about whether we should be eating kosher foods and sacrificing bulls again. We never did that in the first place! But we have our own set of dead works we fall back on.

I know I start to walk by sight again. I rely on logic instead of listening for God's leading. I start reacting to people and situations the way I did before I was a Christian. It's a subtle shift, but it's also a sign that my love relationship with the Lord is dying. I become dependent on my reasoning and not my relationship with God.

But God doesn't want me to depend on my so-called knowledge. He wants me to depend on him. So whenever I think I've got God figured out, he does things in a way I haven't seen before. He does that to get my attention and keep me dependent on him and not on my own "spiritual knowledge."

That doesn't mean God is constantly changing or evolving so that I can't know him. It's just that he's so great that I constantly find new sides to him. This ancient newness of God is a paradox—and given our depraved nature, a comfort.

> For my thoughts are not your thoughts, neither are your ways my ways, declares the LORD. As the heavens are higher than the earth, so are my ways higher than your ways and my thoughts than your thoughts.
> —ISAIAH 55:8-9

92

He's the God of Surprises

Imagine an ant trying to figure out human beings. The ant sees us do something one way once, and he makes a religion out of it. He becomes an expert on us: "Oh, yes," he tells the other ants, "that woman will come out of that building when the sun goes down. She'll get in that thing with wheels and it will take her away."

So one day some of us go outside at noon to get the mail, and there goes the ant's theology. Ruined! He feels like we've failed him. We didn't do things his way. All the other ants respected him as the authority on human beings, and we've made a fool of him.

How often do we do this to God? We try to tame him and fit him into the box of our expectations and understanding. But God is not like a lion in the circus who can be tamed by humans, like a lion in the circus. God is not domesticated. He can't be cornered. He's not a formula or bound by any rules.

Some people say God is bound by his Word, but really his Word is bound by him. He doesn't read our theology books and say to himself, "Okay, I see that I'm allowed to do this, but I had better not do that, because these people I created don't think I would."

No, God is totally free and not required to submit to anyone. He is the creator of everything physical and spiritual.

So why don't we fear him? To fear the Lord means that we never usurp God's role. We never take his place in deciding when, where, or how he's going to act.

Haven't each of us tried to play God, though? For instance, haven't you expected that God will deal with you like he's dealt with another Christian you know? Did you ever consider that God might need to deal with you differently than your neighbors?

He may deal with them with patience and gentleness, so you expect the same, right? But when God comes down hard, don't you say, "Wait a minute, God, what about that guy? You were gentle with him."

"Well," the Lord says, "I am his God and I am your God—and I will treat you justly, but my justice is only understandable to me. Don't try to figure me out, because I work differently in different people's lives. Still, I'm working to the same end. I'm just going to get there different ways."

See, we can't know how God is going to do something. But we can trust God's character. We can always know that his motives are love, mercy, and bringing people to repentance. So while we can't predict how God will demonstrate it, we can depend on his love for us.

Isn't that kind of mercy and justice surprising?

93

KEEPING THE FAITH
BY KEEPING IT FRESH

The Pharisees were an interesting group. They loved to walk around in public with their long beards and their long tassels on their robes. They prayed longer, louder, and more publicly than anybody else. They had more rules and regulations than the Marine Corps. How pompous and ridiculous they looked!

In fact, did you know the Pharisees were the only group of people who drew out Jesus' anger? Jesus had time for society's undesirable lepers, sworn enemies like the Samaritans, despised crooks like the tax collectors, and the brash prostitutes. But what did he say about the Pharisees?

> Woe to you teachers of the law and Pharisees, you hypocrites! You will give a tenth of your spices—mint, dill, and cumin. But you have neglected the more important matters of the law—justice, mercy and faithfulness. You should have practiced the latter, without neglecting the former. You blind guides! You strain out a gnat, but swallow a camel. Woe to you, teachers of the law and Pharisees, you hypocrites! You clean the outside of the cup and dish, but inside they are full of greed and self-indulgence.

—MATTHEW 23:23-25

Can't you picture it? These pompous religious people are out in their gardens, crawling around on the ground counting the leaves on their herb bushes. They use their loudest voices to count, so everyone will know how holy they are as they pick every tenth leaf to tithe to the Lord. Forget about not letting the left hand know what the right hand is doing—these guys let the whole neighborhood know!

It's funny to think of the Pharisees doing these things, but we're all candidates for becoming just as cold-hearted.

All we have to do is love the Word of God more than God, or love written truth more than living truth, or want to spend more time pursuing knowledge than the one who gives knowledge. All we have to do is love our blow-out prayer and praise services more than the one who is high and lifted up.

Here's a warning: As true relationship with the Lord becomes less of a priority to us, we learn to imitate spirituality. What about imitating Christ?

Someone once said to me, "If the Holy Spirit left all the churches in America, 90 percent of the church members wouldn't even know he had gone."

If the Holy Spirit left you, how long would it be before you noticed?

That was Jesus' complaint about the church at Ephesus. He said to them, "You and I both know all the great things you're doing. But look, guys, I'm not there with you anymore. Did any of you happen to notice I was gone?"

In the flesh we're like the Pharisees, always trying to reduce relationship to rules. Jesus spoke to the chief religious leaders of his day, saying, "I tell you the truth, the tax collectors and the prostitutes are entering the kingdom of God ahead of you" (Matthew 21:31).

His message to those of us who love the Word of God is this: You know God's Word and all its requirements. You know all the prophecies, every shade of meaning and possible interpretation, but be careful because you may not know me. I came to fulfill the law. If you get stuck on rules and don't know me, then the most rotten sinner has more chance of getting into heaven than you do. But I want you there, too.

What will you do today to stay fresh and warm in your relationship with the Lord?

94

Why God Won't
Settle for a Spin

Recently a man came to visit our ministry and I asked him, "Are you a Christian?"

"Well, kind of," he replied. "I'm what you call a backslidden Christian."

"But that's worse than an outright sinner," I told him.

"I don't think it's that bad," he said. "I'm not immoral or anything. I still believe in God. It's just that there are some things I'm not ready to give up yet."

He approached being a Christian as if he were buying a new car. You know, you go into the dealership to check out the option packages. On Option One there are cloth seats and a fancy stereo. Option Two comes with leather seats and a four-speed transmission, and so on.

Well, when you become Christian, you may think you can check out the options, that there's the Savior-Only Option, the Lordship Option, the Backslidden Option.

"Ah, that's the option I want," you might say. "The Backslidden Option lets me do everything I want and still call myself a Christian. If I like the ride, I can take up the Savior-Only Option or the Lordship package later."

But there are no options when taking up Christ. You either make him Lord of your life or by not doing so, you sin and compromise. You can't be called a Christian without living like one. To do otherwise is just making excuses. You can't trick your way into heaven. God isn't fooled. You can't get to the final judgment, then start calling Jesus "Lord" and hope to get into heaven. Lordship is something that is worked out here on earth. Jesus said:

> Not everyone who says to me "Lord, Lord" will enter the kingdom of heaven, but only he who does the will of my Father who is in heaven.
> —MATTHEW 7:21

The New Testament always talks about making Jesus Lord, not simply Savior.

What makes you a Christian? Are you relying on the name, or are your actions a mirror of Christ's actions? Do they clearly demonstrate his lordship over your life?

95

Why "Do" and "Go" Are Part of "God"

We love to read the New Testament and note words like "blessed," "receive," "gift," "promise," and "reward." But not many of us like to note the word "do." In fact, the word "do" has been neglected by Christians today because "do" sounds like work, commitment, and having to make difficult choices.

It is each of those things.

When you read the Bible, there is no way you can get away from the call "to do" because doing is the outworking of Lordship. By doing what he commands you to do, you prove to all that Christ, not you, sits on the throne of authority in your life. You surrender control of every area to him, come under his authority, and acknowledge his authority is supreme. You start taking orders from him, and you do what he tells you to do. That's what Lordship is—Christ reigning as supreme authority over your life. So making Jesus Lord is not something passive. It's not a state of being.

Jesus' words challenge us simply and clearly on this matter: "Why do you call me 'Lord, Lord,' and don't do what I say?" So as Christians we are called to action.

Do not merely listen to the word, and so deceive yourselves. Do what it says. Anyone who listens to the word but does not do what it says is like a man who looks at his face in a mirror and, after looking at himself, goes away and immediately forgets what he looks like. But the man who looks intently into the perfect law that gives freedom, and continues to do this, not forgetting what he has heard, but doing it—he will be blessed in what he does.

—JAMES 1:22-25

Have you been too stuffy or too selfish to get out and do what Jesus clearly told you to do? Or do you want to take seriously that little two-letter word "do" and another one that Jesus commanded? That's right: "Go."

96

READY FOR TAKE-OFF?

One time, as Melody and I were flying back from a concert, I led the guy sitting next to me on the plane to the Lord. After we landed, this guy went to the airport bathroom, flushed the drugs he'd been abusing down the toilet, then looked at me and asked, "Now what do I do?"

Good question.

What was I going to do? Was I going to say to him, "Well, praise God. Here's a gospel tract and the phone number for the church office. The office is open from 9:00 A.M. to 5:00 P.M., Monday through Friday, so if you run into difficulties, just call them. Well, good luck and praise God!"

I couldn't say that. I couldn't send this baby Christian back to the drug houses where he'd lived. He needed a fresh start, fellowship, discipleship.

I knew the written Word of God and as I pondered it I heard the Lord whisper, "If a man needs food, feed him. If he needs clothes, clothe him. If you have done it to the least, or the most new, of my brethren you have done it to me." I knew the Lord wanted me to invite this new Christian to come stay with Melody and me so we could help him get established in his relationship to God.

My human nature, however, wasn't happy about what was happening. It wanted to get back on the throne and exercise a little authority. It screamed at me: "Where will he sleep? Do you want to take financial responsibility for him until he gets a job? What if he won't get a job? Besides, you have enough to do. God is using you in other important ways. You don't want to get bogged down ministering to a guy you met on an airplane."

But God had spoken. I knew what to do, and soon we were on our way home with this newly converted guy riding along in the backseat.

So that, I learned, is how we become doers of the Word: by being sensitive to the voice of the Lord when he speaks to us, and by doing exactly what he tells us to do.

97

BE ALL
THAT YOU ARE

It doesn't make any sense to be a Christian and not be a Christian; to call Jesus Lord, but not do what he says. In fact, saying you're a Christian when you aren't willing to open your home or sacrifice your time, energy, money, and possessions, is like saying to God, "I know you're my Lord, but I can't act like you're my Lord. I can't do the things you want me to do, or sacrifice the things you've commanded me to sacrifice. But bless your name because you're my Lord."

It's the same as saying to your husband or wife, "I know I'm your spouse. I have a certificate to prove it. But I can't live with you, take care of you, spend time with you, or sleep with you. Praise God for our commitment to each other, though. Praise God for our marriage."

Sounds crazy, doesn't it? So why is it that too many of us say exactly that to God with our actions?

I, for one, am guilty of that. Like the foolish man who built his house without a foundation, which Jesus talked about in Luke 6, I hadn't paid proper attention to the foundations of my relationship with him. So God had to deal with me on the whole issue of Lordship.

One day I became conscious of him speaking into my heart: "Keith, why do you call me, 'Lord, Lord,' but don't do what I've asked? There are people in your neighborhood who you haven't even talked to yet."

"Well, I haven't felt you leading me to talk to them," I answered the Lord. I wasn't ready for his reply.

"What's all this about 'feeling led,' Keith? Where did you get that idea? Doesn't my Word say 'Go into all the world and preach the gospel to every creature'? You haven't done what I clearly told you to do."

"But, Lord," I began reasoning, "I've got to be realistic about things. I can't do all that right now. I have my family to take care of, and if I don't get enough sleep and relaxation my whole ministry will suffer."

Then the Lord said to me: "It's not your ministry, Keith. It's mine. I gave it to you to be a steward over. I don't want you to win the whole world to me. All I want you to do is what you can. But you're not doing that yet. You're not doing what I commanded. You keep usurping the authority you gave to me."

When I heard these words from the Lord, I broke down and wept. He was right. I was good at calling him "Lord," but I wasn't living like he was my Lord.

A girl wrote me a poem recently. One of the lines said, "It isn't the ship in the water that sinks the ship. It's the water in the ship that sinks the ship."

It's the same with you and me. We can make Jesus Lord of our lives or allow anything else in the world to compromise Christ's Lordship. But it isn't the Christian in the world that creates problems—it's the world in the Christian.

98

How Broken Is Blest?

The Bible teaches that either we take seriously and submit to the Lordship of Christ, allowing him to reshape us and transform our lives into his image, or we will be crushed eventually and destroyed through our lack of obedience.

Unfortunately, many Christians across the nation are asleep. We've been lulled by the message that says we're doing fine, that the Lord is pleased with us, that all we need to do is hold on because Jesus is coming back for us soon.

For a while I was lulled by this message. That is, until I read in Revelation the letters to the seven churches. These churches seemed to have things together a whole lot better than I did, but God took a tough stand against them.

So how come the only message I was hearing was that God was pleased with me?

I didn't have to wait long for an answer. The Lord spoke directly to my heart: "Keith, you're not listening to the right message. You're listening to the bless-me gospel. I want to mold your life after me, not modern Christianity. I want to be your Lord, but you must surrender that place of authority to me. I won't take it by force. I want your willing submission and obedience."

Jesus said, "He who falls on this stone will be broken to pieces, but he on whom it falls will be crushed" (Matthew 21:44). He challenges me to be broken before him, including every talent, opportunity, and thing I possess. That means surrendering it all to him.

Now, it's not wrong to go to college, get married, or own a house or a business, but all of these things need to be laid before Jesus. Like the loaves and fishes at the feeding of the 5,000 (Matthew 14:13-21), they need to be blessed and broken by God.

After all, Jesus told the seven churches: You can be broken now or broken later.

> To him who overcomes and does my will to the end, I will give authority over the nations—"He will rule them with an iron scepter; he will dash them to pieces like pottery"—just as I have received authority from my Father. I will also give him the morning star. He who has an ear, let him hear what the Spirit says to the churches.
>
> —REVELATION 2:26-29

99

You Do the Math

I heard a story once about a beggar in India. This man had been begging all day long and had only a half-cup of rice to show for it. As he was rolling up his begging mat, preparing to go home, he heard the sound of the army approaching. The prince was coming! So the beggar sat down again and waited.

Just as the prince was about to pass, his highness stopped, climbed down from his elephant, went over to the beggar, and asked for some rice.

The beggar simply stared. *What nerve!* he thought. *The prince wants my rice when he can afford to buy sacks of rice—and he wants me to give up my little cup!*

Yet not wanting to refuse the prince or wanting to give up too much of his rice, the beggar counted out three grains and handed them over.

Graciously, the prince took the grains of rice and showed them to his head servant. As the prince moved on, the head servant walked over and dropped three gold coins in the beggar's lap. When the beggar saw the coins, he ran after the procession, offering the rest of the rice. If he had known he was going to get a gold coin for every grain of rice, he gladly would have given it all. But now, the opportunity passed, nobody took notice of him.

The prince of heaven wants us to exchange all that we cling to for immeasurable riches. Are we going to make the same mistake as this beggar and hold back?

Too often we do. We are beggars who want to hold some back—"in case things don't work out," we tell ourselves. We keep a little authority over our lives, just to be sure. But Jesus fed 5,000 people with a few loaves of bread and two fish. If we would give all of ourselves to him, think of what he could do with us.

100

Give Back What's His

People like my singing and piano playing. But when I became a Christian, the Lord asked me to lay down my music. I'd have been a fool to cling to it. What's my talent compared to the one who fashioned the universe? What's my most creative thought compared to the creativity of the one who formed me from dust? So I did lay down my music, not knowing if God would ever want me to play and sing again.

Of course it was a struggle. It made me wonder why we Christians are so reluctant to hand over our lives completely to God anyway. Why do we refuse to give God, who gave us everything, what he asks?

God desires people who will make him Lord over their lives—not in lip service, but in reality; not just in what they say, but in what they do.

If making Jesus the Lord of our lives is not of utmost importance to us, then we're wasting our time—and God's. In Revelation, Jesus says to the church at Laodicea:

> I know your deeds, that you are neither cold nor hot. I wish you were either one or the other! So because you are lukewarm—neither hot nor cold—I am about to spit you out of my mouth.
> —Revelation 3:15-16

It's time to evaluate your commitment to Christ. Only a life totally committed to God can answer his challenge: "Why do you call me 'Lord, Lord,' and do not do what I say?"

Are you a Christian merely in what you say or in what you do, too? Are you a person who can say wholeheartedly, "Jesus is my Lord"? Like the parable in Luke 6:46-49, where the wise builder digs deep to lay a solid foundation, we must dig deep in our lives and lay a solid foundation of Lordship. The matter is simple: If Jesus is not Lord of all, then he's not Lord at all.

LAST DAYS MINISTRIES INFORMATION

↜LAST DAYS MINISTRIES↝

Visit our website: www.lastdaysministries.org

Who We Are

Just as the music and writings of Keith Green continue as an inheritance to this generation, so does Last Days Ministries. LDM was founded in 1977 by Keith and Melody Green. After Keith went to be with Jesus, Melody continued their ministry. LDM is committed to the Lord Jesus and to reaching the world with God's love.

Our Goal

To the best of our ability to express the things that are on the Lord's heart for the hour we live in—to emphasize the topics and issues we feel God wants us to highlight.

Our Mission

To challenge and encourage believers to pursue an uncompromising love for Jesus and an active faith that puts feet to their prayers to impact the world. We believe the church is called to disciple Christians and that Christians are called beyond the walls of the church to reach the poor, the hurting, and the lost—in their communities and in foreign lands.

Our Desire

We desire to see believers loving and worshiping God while fulfilling their calls and destinies regardless of gender, age, or nationality.

∾www.lastdaysministries.org∾

A place of inspiration, learning, networking, mission, Christian growth, and finding Jesus.

Keith Green
> Learn more about the ministry and music of this intense young man whose brief life keeps touching millions around the world.

Melody Green
> Ministry Travel Schedule
> Melody's Monthly Message and Commentary
> Online Chats with Melody

Free Downloads!
> Hundreds of life-changing articles on relevant topics by:
>> Keith Green
>> Melody Green
>> John Dawson
>> Floyd McClung
>> Winkie Pratney
>> Leonard Ravenhill
>> and many others

Special Features, including:
> 4 Youth by Youth
> Women in Ministry
> Missions—Into the Nations, into the Streets
> Hot Topics for Today's Christians
> How to Find God

❧LAST DAYS MINISTRIES RESOURCES❧

Order from Last Days Ministries Online at
www.lastdaysministries.org

Special Keith Green Materials

*New Keith Green TV Documentary Available
on Video*
What made Keith tick? A high-quality, com-
prehensive, candid history of Keith's life and
ministry. Includes concert and preaching
footage, personal photos, memories from
family, friends, and musical peers.

Keith Green Memorial Concert Video
Includes a 25-minute excerpt from one of
Keith's last concerts, home movies, plus
Melody's account of the plane crash and
God's mercy since then. Shown around the
world with powerful results.

The Music of Keith Green
If you haven't heard Keith's music you
haven't heard his heart. Log on to www.last-
daysministries.org to listen to songs that
reveal Keith's passion for God and his powerful gift of music.

Books by and about Keith Green
*If You Love the Lord: Uncompromising Devotions
from the Heart of Keith Green* by Keith Green

A special collection of Keith Green devotions (adapted from *A Cry in the Wilderness*).

No Compromise: The Life Story of Keith Green (expanded edition) by Melody Green and David Hazard

A fascinating, in-depth glimpse into Keith's heart, music, and life.

LDM Ministry Materials

Concert videos, teaching tapes, and special offerings by Keith Green, Melody Green, and other LDM favorites (many available only through LDM).

Worship Music

Powerful Books

Inspiring Art

Giveaways

and much, much more!

No Compromise (Revised and Expanded)
By Melody Green with David Hazard

"Keith was uncompromising in his call to holiness, even when it made the rest of us uncomfortable. Now years after his death his music still affects us all."

—Amy Grant

Longtime fans and new listeners can experience the impact of Keith's character, courage, and commitment in this revised and expanded testimony of his extraordinary life.

Who better to tell Keith Green's story than the woman who shared his life and mission—his wife, Melody. At the time Keith and two of their children were killed in a tragic plane crash, Melody was pregnant and had a one-year-old child at home. She inherited Keith's musical legacy of published and unpublished songs and his private journals, which she has put together in this extremely personal biography of Keith.